Dedication

Dear Heavenly Father,
I ask that you bless this humble work of mine.

That you would use it to bless and
encourage those who read it.

That it would be of great benefit to them.

"Do everything for the glory of God,
even your eating and drinking."
I Corinthians 10:31 (Living Bible)

Low Carb Cooking at Sharron's Place

Sugar Free Recipes Featuring SteviaPlus®

Written and Illustrated by Sharron Long

Humility Publications

Humility Publications
PO Box 835
Washougal, WA 98671

The author may be contacted at:
www.Sharrons-Place.com (please note the dash) or by email at Sharron@lowcarbeating.com .
To learn more about SteviaPlus® Fiber, please visit www.wisdomherbs.com.
For more information about low carb diets, please visit www.lowcarbeating.com.

The advice offered in this book is based upon the author's own experience and is not meant to replace your doctor's counsel. If you are experiencing health problems, please see your doctor.

Table of Contents

Introduction

Tips & Techniques

Breakfasts

Main Courses

Veggies, Sides and Snacks

Salads Dressings and Sauces

Desserts

Sugar-Free, Non-Low Carb Recipes

Appendixes

Introduction

COME ON IN!

Welcome to my place! I'm so glad you could come! Can I get you something to drink? I have some freshly brewed licorice-spice sun-tea in the `fridge. Lots of ice? That sounds good to me, too. It's been really hot today.

Come sit down and relax. Let's enjoy our tea.

How much weight have I lost? Well, as of right now, I've lost 70 pounds. I've lost 47 pounds since being on the Atkins diet. I have about 25 pounds to go to reach my goal.

I'm feeling really good, but it has really been a process. I can't say that just "this" or just "that" has been what has helped me the most. It all seems to be working together to form a whole. Like the pieces of a puzzle or the elements of a design. I'd say low carbing is the background of the picture of what I'm doing. Then come the different layers: Dealing with the candida infection I had, treating the fibromyalgia, eliminating food allergies. All those things have each built upon the other to the point where I am actually feeling quite well!

The other day, I had just sat down at the dinner table with my family and realized that I had accomplished a phenomenal amount in just a little over one hour's time. I had driven to the store to buy lighter fluid for the barbecue, gathered, sorted and started the laundry, cooked dinner on the barbecue, and prepared a protein dish to have for dinner the following night. I did some writing, washed the hand-washing dishes, and then sat down to enjoy my dinner. I was NOT exhausted! A year ago, I could NEVER have done a fraction of that and still been functioning at all! What an incredible feeling!

LOW CARB EATING

The first layer in the design is the low carb diet. By diet, I do not mean calorie-restriction! I simply mean a way of eating.

My family had been under extreme stress. My husband had lost a dream job, and we were struggling through all the repercussions. He had to return to work as a cabinetmaker, in humility. It was an extremely difficult time for us. On a Friday evening in January, 2001, while dining out with my family at a favorite burger place, I had a horrible dizzy spell. My face and arm went numb. I was afraid I'd had a stroke! Later, I called the help line for my insurance company and spoke with the nurse on duty. She assured me, she didn't think I'd had a stroke. She did want me to go see the doctor first thing Monday. I could feel my neck was out of place, so I chose to see my chiropractor.

When I saw my doctor the next morning, he asked about the work situation and checked my blood pressure. It spiked to 172/92! Within two minutes it had returned to a somewhat lower number, but was still quite high. He freaked out! He was waving his arms at me and yelling – out of his extreme concern over my situation. He feared I'd be dead within five years.

For sometime he'd been wanting me to go on the Atkin's low carb diet. I had been extremely resistant, to put it mildly. Quite frankly, I did not want to give up my carbs! Two other doctors had wanted to restrict my carbohydrate intake over the years, and I hadn't listened to them either. I truly was addicted.

This time, though, he would not take "no" for an answer. He insisted. He spelled out exactly what he wanted me to do and told me to go to the library and get the book, <u>Dr. Atkin's New Diet Revolution.</u>

I did well on induction, the initial "withdrawl" phase of the diet where carbohydrates are limited to 20 grams or less per day. I lost about 10 pounds in the two weeks, and my blood pressure leveled out at 100/70.

I didn't lose as I'd hoped. It took two months for me to lose four pounds. Then the ball dropped...

CANDIDA
I had been taking allergy shots for about a year and a half at that time. I always reacted to the shots with large, red welts at the injection site.

On March 27, 2001, while in the allergist's office, I saw my chart. On it, in big, bold letters, was the word, "Candida." My eyes gaped. My mouth fell. My heart dropped. Aghast, I said, "Candida?!?" The injection nurse glanced up at me and calmly said, though it were the simplest thing in the world, "Oh, yes, we're treating you for candida!"

I felt as if my world had fallen apart. Candida! I have a friend who was treated for candida many years ago. The treatment left her paralyzed. She still cannot walk to this day. The thought of candida struck fear in my heart.

I re-read Dr. Atkin's chapter on Candida, checked out Dr. Crook's, <u>Chronic Fatigue and the Yeast Connection</u> from the library and searched on the Internet for information. It took a lot of sifting through a huge amount of information to really find what I needed to know on the subject.

I began taking oil of oregano and acidophilus. I learned I needed to make more dietary changes. It was difficult, but I eliminated all dairy products (including cheese), vinegar, mushrooms, soy sauce, all forms of sugar (including fruit), peanuts, pistachios and wheat from my already restricted diet. An acquaintance sternly warned me that she had "almost killed herself by self-treating," and I needed to be under a doctor's care.

I knew I did not want to go to my primary-care doctor. He had already prescribed anti-depressants to me on two or three different occasions. Who knew how he would react to this!? I made an appointment with a local naturopathic chiropractor.

Prior to the appointment, I spent a couple of hours writing a detailed medical history of myself. I didn't want to hide anything. I wanted him to know the severity and extent of all my symptoms. Previously, anytime I had been even vaguely honest with a doctor about my symptoms, they had prescribed anti-depressants. I had always reacted badly to the medication. Besides, I wasn't depressed. I was sick. I was tired. I hurt everywhere. I didn't sleep well at night. I was grouchy with my family and wasn't losing the weight as I had hoped. I wanted adequate treatment. I didn't need anti-depressants, I needed relief!

The doctor read my history and commented, "This reads like a bad novel!" He took thorough notes and then made his recommendations. I was to continue the oil of oregano as my primary medication to fight the candida, and he gave me a stronger acidophilus blend.

On a subsequent visit, I complained about how grouchy I'd been with my children. He asked about my sleeping patterns and pain level. He said he could give me something to help me sleep, but he really didn't think that was the problem.

FIBROMYALGIA (CHRONIC FATIGUE SYNDROME)
He said he felt I had fibromyalgia, (also called chronic fatigue syndrome), and if we could get the pain under control, I would sleep better and not be so grumpy.

Tears came to my eyes. Finally, a doctor that was really listening to me! One that heard my problems and didn't just try to slap me with an anti-depressant! Now, I could see a light at the end of the tunnel.

He had me take a prescription strength malic acid formula. He explained that the malic acid was supposed to break the pain and fatigue cycle that goes with fibromyalgia.

I did more research on the internet and learned that studies have shown people with fibromyalgia don't produce malic acid on their own. Malic acid is normally produced during exercise. It aids muscles in healing from the wear and tear that happens during exercise. Folks who have fibromyalgia don't produce this acid, so it causes the pain and fatigue cycle that is one of the hallmarks of fibromyalgia.

I began by taking just 1/2 teaspoon (450 mg) of the malic acid combination daily and have increased to a total of 1800 mg daily. I noticed an improvement in my pain level.

Another product I recently added to my supplement routine is colloidal minerals. Within 24 hours of starting them, I noticed a dramatic pain reduction in my back. Drinking a lot of water and adequate salt intake helps keep the pain in check, as well. Yet, I have also discovered another piece of the puzzle...

ALLERGIES
My symptoms had gotten worse again. I was grouchy, aching and tired. I was needing one and a half to two hour long naps

each day and impatient and snappish with my children. I felt sluggish and bloated. It had been a gradual change, but I had definitely noticed the change. Where had all the energy gone?

I keep a weight loss and measurement log. I usually weigh daily and measure weekly. It has given me help in determining which foods I can tolerate and which I can't. I am usually bloated by 2 to 4 pounds the following morning after eating something that my system does not like!

That log has really helped me in this discovery process. I knew I had allergies. In fact, my allergist once looked at me with eyes opened wide with concern and told me, "You are HIGHLY allergic!" He treats for environmental allergies, like dust and mold, but he won't even test for food intolerances. He has left the sleuthing to me! Lucky me...

I had noticed that I didn't feel as well when we had eaten chicken, but I wasn't sure. It wasn't a violent reaction... Yet.

I eliminated chicken from my diet for about a week, then had barbecue chicken for a late dinner one night. The next morning, I could hardly walk! My head felt as if it was full of cobwebs, and I could barely say a discernable sentence. I couldn't think straight at all or do anything until after I had eaten some breakfast. I felt miserable! It was the first time in several weeks that I had felt that way.

I decided I would avoid chicken for a while longer and see what happened. I felt good. I had a good energy level, and I was having fun with my children. I was being creative and generally enjoying life.

Then I had chicken for lunch one day. I laid down for a rest and slept overly long. I woke up feeling miserable. My head hurt. I was extremely grumpy with my children. My legs and arms felt like lead. Pain was shooting down my right leg, the heels of both feet were numb, and I was having trouble speaking. My husband gave me a dose of oil of oregano, (it is an allergy relief medicine as well as candida aid), and I laid down on the couch. In a few minutes, my head began to clear. After eating, another hour or so passed, and I began feeling better.

I won't be eating chicken again for a long time!

I spoke with my doctor about this episode. I told him how all my fibromyalgia symptoms were full blown and very extreme after eating the chicken and asked him if fibromyalgia and allergies were linked. He said, "A lot of people wonder around not knowing if they are sick with the flu or having some serious problems. A lot of other often serious conditions can be linked to allergies."

ARE YOU BOTHERED BY ALLERGIES OR FIBROMYALGIA (CHRONIC FATIGUE)?

You may be wondering how to know if candida or allergies are an issue in your life? Not everyone can have an allergy test for candida. How can you find out? A certain medical doctor has written several books about the subject. While I do not agree with his dietary recommendations, (he recommends the old high-carb, low-fat diet), I would begin by going to the library and checking out Dr. Crook's <u>Chronic Fatigue and the Yeast Connection</u>. It will be able to answer questions I cannot. I am not a doctor, just a sufferer.

I can ask a few questions to get you thinking: Are you often bothered by unexplainable symptoms, like fatigue and moodiness? Do you get frequent infections, like sinus, bladder or yeast? Do you have frequent colds or flu symptoms? If you have any of these, I would strongly suggest that you find a qualified Naturopathic Physician. He or she would be able to provide the most comprehensive care. In my experience, a regular Medical Doctor is not likely to be able to either diagnose or treat these symptoms adequately.

WHAT ABOUT MY FAMILY?

When I first went on the Atkin's plan, I began to notice the way the rest of my family was eating. Or should I say, the way I was feeding them? They ate the typical very high carbohydrate diet that I think every typical American family eats! Lots of noodles, macaroni and cheese and rice. I did some serious thinking and asked many, many questions of the folks on the message boards at www.lowcarbeating.com who had been on this eating plan for some time.

What I've done with my family is seriously increased their protein consumption. I make sure they have a good protein source at every meal, even if it is only hot dogs. We no longer have chips, except pork rinds, and I only buy 100% whole wheat bread and whole grain crackers. I don't buy any of the sugar-sweetened treats.

I've discovered my five year old son, Aaron, has an allergy to sugar. I began to suspect the allergy after reading in Dr. Crook's book that allergies can cause hyperactive type behavior, especially in young children. Some days he would be the most wonderful, sweet, kind, helpful little boy anyone would ever want to meet! Other days, he was a wild, out-of-control, crazed thing! He would literally bounce off the walls for a while, then end up laying on the floor moaning, crying and sucking his fingers asking to go to bed! The thing that seemed to trigger it was sugar.

We went for a week with absolutely no sugar (cane or beet type, brown or white). Then a friend gave gave my kids lunch. Aaron was wild! He had been given peanut butter and jam sandwiches, (that were mostly jam), for lunch. Within 20 minutes, he had "crashed." All I could do was cuddle him, pray for him and put him to bed. It was awful.

We have also discovered he is allergic to wheat by eliminating it, then reintroducing it in a controlled situation.

Since then I have adapted some of my recipes to be "normal" but sugar and wheat free. I've made some desserts and other items for the other family members that are not low carb, but are sugar and wheat free. This way, I can send "treats" with my kids, particularly Aaron, to places where he will need such things. He won't feel left out when the other kids are having dessert, and I know he won't end up being sick for it! It has really helped a lot.

By reducing the processed foods in my family's diet and increasing their protein intake, as well as adding good quality supplements, I've seen a dramatic improvement in their health! My whole family has become extremely healthy. Bad viruses have gone around, but not at our home! My kids have all been having serious growing spurts and my husband is finely well.

My husbands had been living on a very high carb, highly processed, high sugar diet. He ate cereal with lots of milk and sugar every day. Each day for lunch he ate a peanut butter and jelly sandwich, potato chips, a fried fruit pie, carrots and a banana. He was getting sick every two weeks just like clock-work! After a life-time of being extremely healthy, his immune system was way down and the doctor said he looked as if he had developed allergies. He gave him medication, which slightly helped the symptoms, and made him slightly groggy! That is very dangerous in his line of work! It didn't keep the symptoms from returning, either.

We changed his breakfast to eggs and his lunch to include two meat sandwiches on 100% whole wheat bread, olives, peanuts, and often either carrots or a piece of fruit. He had been taking a multi-vitamin and a B-complex vitamin. We added an anti-oxidant formula to his supplements. That has done it! He has not been sick for months. What a blessing!

If you have questions about my family's progress, you may visit me on the web at www.Sharrons-Place.com and check out the cooking forum at www.lowcarbeating.com. I'm as close as an email or post to the message board.

Tips and Techniques

HERB GARDENING

Shall we look at my herb garden? You say you don't know the first thing about gardening? I am just learning as I go, just like everything else. I have found that planting herbs in large pots is very convenient and even a person in an apartment could grow cooking herbs if they get a little bit of sun in a window!

My favorites are lemon-thyme and chives. I also have mint, rosemary, thyme and a tiny little oregano plant. The mint and lemon-thyme are thriving in their containers! I purchased big pots, probably 3 to 5 gallons each for my herbs.

I also have a few edible flowers around. Yes, edible flowers! Nasturtium blossoms have a peppery taste rather like radishes, pansies taste like, well, pansies! Rose petals are also edible, and, of course, they taste like roses.

What does a lemon-thyme taste like? It has a wonderful lemony smell and taste combined with something like a mild mint. It doesn't taste at all like a normal thyme plant to me. It is my absolute favorite herb to make something taste "special," like for company coming. Chives are very useful as is parsley. Parsley is my staple herb. I think I use it in almost every savory dish I make!

Did you know that herbs need hair-cuts just like kids do? At least that is what I call it! I go out with my big kitchen scissors and a big plastic grocery bag and give them a trim every couple of months. That encourages new growth in the plants and also discourages them going to seed. I only put in my bag the tender cuttings, not the old brown leaves or ones with flowers. Then I bring them inside, give them a good bath in my sink full of cold water and stick them in my food dehydrator for a couple of hours. At the end of the time, I remove the leaves from the stems and put them in little jars for future use. I've just done two things for myself: I've given myself herbs for use when the plants are dormant during the winter and encouraged healthier plants! What more could I ask for?

You don't think you could grow herbs? Really, if I can do it anyone can! I've done it from seed before, but the easiest way I've found is just to go to my local hardware store's garden center and choose the ones I want. The best way for me is to purchase them already started, sure I'm spending a bit more, but none of these plants are expensive! The most expensive one I have still cost me less than $2.00.

You just need some fairly large pots, at least a gallon in size, some rocks, broken pottery or bricks, or old pieces of wood and potting soil. I also use a powdered fertilizer that is for use on garden herbs. I keep it mixed up in an old gallon milk jug that I've washed and labeled for that purpose. I've even discovered a cheap plastic bucket, the kind that kid's toys are often stored in, will work well if the plant is moisture loving! I've had a mint plant for three years now. It was in a well drained wooden planter. That planter fell apart this spring, and all I could afford was the bucket. Mint grows in the wild in really wet conditions, so I figured it would be okay. It is doing fabulously well!

All you have to do is place the broken bits of clay, bricks, etc., in the bottom of the pot. They provide drainage for any excess moisture. For a very large pot, like my 10 gallon bucket that has the mint in it, I filled it about 1/4 with the bits and pieces of bricks and wood. For a smaller pot, just a couple of inches will do. Then pile in the potting soil to with in a few inches of the top. Make a well in the soil, pour in lots of water mixed with the fertilizer, remove the plant from the store's container, plunk it in and keep it moist. Water every day for the first week or so, then just don't let it get all dried out.

I can't tell you how many dishes have gone from being just good to being spectacular by adding just a pinch of fresh herbs. It's worth it, even if you live in the city or in an apartment. Just keep them like you would any house plant. They are definitely worth the effort expended!

BARBECUING

During the warmer months, I hardly cook meat in the oven! I don't like to heat up the house, and the flavor of barbecued meat is just beyond compare.

I prefer to use a combination of normal briquettes and mesquite chunks. There is a type of coal that is pure mesquite, and I find the food is best flavored when I use two or three chunks of mesquite mixed in with the normal coals. The briquettes that have mesquite mixed into them are fine, but the pure mesquite way gives the food a superior flavor.

Do you ever have trouble lighting the coals? Boy, I sure do! If you live in a high humidity area, the following is the method I have found that works the best, (and believe me I've tried a lot!): Open all the vents on the barbecue to their largest positions. Then, thoroughly soak the coals with barbecue lighter fluid. Set a timer for 5 minutes. No more, no less. Any changes just don't seem to work! When the timer goes off, light the coals. They usually light perfectly, unless of course the barbecue needed to be cleaned. I then set the timer for 10 minutes and check them again to make sure they are well lit. 99% of the time, if I use this method, the coals are ready to cook with at this point!

Because the coals are in a pile, they have to be moved. I use stainless steel tongs with a cool-grip handle to spread the coals out evenly over the cooking surface. I have tried various placements of the coal, diffused heat, banking, etc., but I prefer them just laid out in an even layer across the bottom of the cooker. It provides a more even heat, and I like the smoked, grilled flavor.

Ahhh, the smoke! That is what is so wonderful about barbecuing! The smokier it is, the more flavorful the food will be. I actually do my seasoning over the coals, so that the excess herbs and seasonings will fall on the hot coals for an extra smokey flavor. I just sprinkle away, close the barbecue cover tightly, and let it do it's job! If I see it is smoking excessively, I check the meat. I certainly don't want to burn it! If the coals are too hot, the meat can either be moved to the edges of the barbecue, where the heat is less intense, or the fire can actually be "turned down" by closing the air vents on the bottom of the barbecue for a couple of minutes. I just have to remember to reopen them! Otherwise, the fire will smother and the food will be raw. Not a pretty picture.

To make barbecuing more economical, I close the vents when I am finished cooking. Coals aren't that inexpensive. When I am done with whatever I have cooked, I simply close all the vents completely. This smothers the fire and allows me to re-use any coals that are still good. I just gather them back into a pile and light as I've already described.

CHOOSING YOUR POTS AND PANS
When I am not barbecuing, I have to use pots and pans like everyone else. My current favorite type of pans are simple, basic, cast iron! I also have a stove-top wok that gets regular use. The non-stick cookware that has been popular since I've been an adult certainly leaves a lot to be desired. It was developed with the low-fat way of life in mind. It pits and is so fussy about what type of utensils can be used on it. Cast iron is so forgiving! Any utensil can be used, and iron is an element in our bodies; so it won't hurt us if it does flake off! Clean up is easy, as long as the pan is well seasoned.

SEASONING YOUR COOKWARE
Seasoned? That is the process which turns a yucky old pan to which everything sticks, into a wonderful cooking utensil!

I purchased a very inexpensive wok at a thrift store. It was shiny and bright, except where the previous owner had cooked something that had left a burn-stain. I had a lady-friend from the Phillippines, and she taught me how to season it. The process is the same for a wok as it is cast-iron, only a different type of oil is used. A wok will be seasoned with sesame or peanut oil, while a cast-iron pan is seasoned with canola oil, bacon drippings or lard. Olive oil and butter are not suitable for use with intense heat, so they cannot be used to season cookware. Save the olive oil to season your wooden cutting board, and just enjoy the butter!

To season the wok or cast-iron pan, begin with a clean pan. Scrub it as clean as possible. If there are any really stuck-on bits, don't worry, they will burn off during the seasoning process. Using a folded up paper towel (or two if they are thin), rub a small amount of oil onto the entire cooking surface, so that the oil is absorbed by the pan. Turn the heat on to "high" and continue to rub the oil into the pan. Be very careful not to burn your fingers! Keep that towel between you and the hot pan, or you'll end up with a nasty burn. When the pan begins to smoke slightly, turn off the heat and allow the pan to cool. When it is completely cooled, repeat the process. Continue to repeat the above process until the pan has achieved a deep-black, shiny appearance. Once that is done, clean up will only consist of wiping the pan clean with a towel, rubbing a little oil into the surface, bringing it to smoking-heat again and allowing it cool again. Occasionally it will need to be soaked and scrubbed, but then simply repeat the seasoning steps a couple of times and it will be good to go again!

If you have a wooden cutting board, it can be seasoned nicely with olive oil. I have the blessing of a cabinet-maker for a husband. He made me a wonderful "butcher block" type cutting board. It is absolutely gorgeous! To keep it that way, I season it with olive oil periodically. I simply make sure it is clean and dry, then I pour a small amount of olive oil onto the surface. Using a circular motion, I rub the oil into the surface of the board with a clean, dry paper towel. I make sure and cover every area with oil: Bottom, top, sides. I continue the process until no more oil will be absorbed by the board. It forms a layer of oil that just won't soak in any more! After I have used the cutting board, I clean it gently with soap and water, re-seasoning if necessary when dry. I've had my board for about eight years now, and by treating it this way, my board is still in fairly new condition. It will continue to serve our family for years to come.

MORE EQUIPMENT
I've found that my blender and food processor are absolutely indispensable to my way of eating. I really don't know if I would be able to cook the wide variety of foods I prepare with out either of them!

I use my blender to make salad dressings, almond milk and shakes. My food processor is often full of pork rinds or almond bits! I use either or both of them almost every single day.

I have a full-sized food processor with chopping blade as well as slicing and shredding blades. I love it! I had a small one, about half size, and it didn't have the power necessary to grind the nuts, especially. My "new" one I got at a yard sale for $5.00. It is probably 15 years old, but it works fabulously! It can grind nuts to flour in just about a minute and making nut butter only takes about two minutes. I use it to slice and shred cabbage, carrots, the filling ingredients for Egg Rolls, and chop nuts, pork rinds and onions.

A good set of measuring cups and spoons is absolutely essential, as well. One that has a different spoon for each size measurement including 1/2 tablespoon and 1/8 teaspoon is invaluable. Measuring cups should have flat bottoms that can rest on a counter without tipping over when empty. A glass liquid measure with both ounces and cups shown is very useful, either one or two cups will do. Also, a small "dietary" scale is very useful. I got one for a dollar at a general merchandise store!

At least two good knives are essential. It is well worth it to go to a professional kitchen supply store or the like to purchase an all purpose kitchen knife and a French Chef's knife. The knives should be made of high quality steel with either a wooden handle that shows the blade being the entire width and length of the blade or a professional molded plastic one will do. I prefer the wooden handle because then I can see what I am getting!

The utility knife, about 10" long with a common looking blade, can be used for almost any slicing task. The French Chef's knife, a large knife, about 15" long, with a wedge-shaped blade, is for chopping. Grasp the handle firmly with your writing hand, and place the other hand gently on the top (flat edge) of the blade to help provide stability and control. Be sure and keep your fingers up! Chop with a rocking motion, using the point of the blade as a pivot. Finely chopped food in a snap! No more tedious paring-knife chopping!

With those knives, a sharpening steel is a very good investment. How else are you going to keep that nice slicing edge if you don't have a steel? The little "gadgets" that are available in the kitchen areas of most stores are only slightly better than worthless and have the great potential to do damage to your knives. A steel, which is a long, rough, steel rod with a handle, will keep those blades nice and sharp! To use, simply slide the cutting edge down the surface of the steel, first one side then the other. For an extremely sharp edge, do the process under slowly running water.

Wash the knives by hand, not in a dishwasher. This will keep them lasting "good as new" for years to come. A good knife is a good investment.

Another thing to get while at that cooking supply store is a meat thermometer. With all the meat we eat on this way of life, it is a really important tool. How else will you know if that burger is cooked past the point where e-coli or other bacteria will live? My favorite thermometer actually has the temperature guideline printed right on the face of the dial. Ham cooks to 160. Well-done beef, as well as veal, pork and lamb cook to 170 and poultry needs to register 180 to be done.

What if you don't have a thermometer, or it gets broken? There are other ways to test the doneness of meat besides a thermometer. You can poke the meat and see if the juices run clear. Another method, if you are cooking a steak, for instance, and want it to be rare, you can use your own hand as a guide. Simply ball your hand up into a fist. Don't squeeze it, just hold it loosely. The big muscle between your index finger and thumb is the gauge. With the hand in a fist and relaxed, poke that muscle with the index finger of your other hand. That muscle feels like what "rare" meat feels like. With the muscle slightly tightened, that is what "medium-rare" feels like. When the fist is squeezed tight, that is how a "well done" piece of meat feels.

Another simple way is to poke something, like a metal skewer, into the center of the piece of meat and put it against your lip. If it feels hot to the touch, it is most likely done.

There are so many things that I could say are "necessary," but entire books have already been written on the subject! These things I've mentioned are the ones I feel are particularly helpful to this way of eating that I've chosen.

PANTRY BASICS
The staples of the low carb way of eating are quite different than low fat or vegetarian! To make things easier, I've given a detailed list in the appendixes, (see Suggested Shopping List, p. 215).

One of the most basic elements is butter. Real, creamy butter, not margarine or some fake imitation butter-flavored spread, is what we use! I try to purchase brands that don't have added coloring. I buy salted butter, simply because we prefer the taste.

Cooking oils are another essential. I use canola oil for my all purpose frying and cooking oil. It has no taste and from what I understand, it doesn't break down into those nasty trans-fats that are linked with all sorts of health problems. I keep sunflower oil on hand for making mayonnaise, and when I run out of canola, I use it as my back-up cooking oil. A canola based cooking oil spray is also important to have available.

I keep olive oil for salad dressings, but I don't fry with it. Both olive oil and butter aren't particularly good for heating because they scorch at a low temperature, but they are wonderful on so many other things! If a buttery flavor is desired in frying, simply combine a heat-stable oil, like canola, with the butter and fry.

I also like to do a lot of Asian-style cooking. At one point, I had read every Chinese cooking book my local library owned! I've also had lessons from a couple of Philippino families. If candida isn't a problem, then a good soy sauce, purchased at an Asian market would be one thing on my list. Unfortunately, the candida keeps me from having anything fermented, so soy sauce is OFF my list. One thing I still stop in for is sesame oil. I purchase the "roasted" sesame oil – it is brown rather than lightly golden – simply because my Asian market doesn't carry the "virgin" variety that is good for cooking. The dark sesame oil, which most of us have access to, is yet another oil that isn't good for high temperatures. I do season my wok with it because the flavor is beyond compare, but really, that is a "no-no." It does smoke at a low temperature. It is primarily used as a seasoning agent in Asian cooking. While I am at the Asian market, I also get a bottle of hot chili oil – it is displayed with the sesame oil. A few drops will go a LONG way! I also like to get sesame seeds while I am there, because they are just so much fun to have around!

If you like spicy or Mexican-style cooking, then you will want to have tomato sauce, canned tomatoes (without sugar, of course!), chili powder, chilies or jalapeno peppers, and cumin. Ground cumin is the quintessential Mexican spice. It is what gives Mexican-style dishes that special richness. Low carb tortillas are nice to have, if they are available in your area. For Italian-style dishes, an Italian seasoning herb blend is vital in addition to the things listed for Mexican-style cooking.

Lemons and limes are another essential element of my kitchen. Hardly a day goes by without me squeezing one for something! I only use the bottled type when I run out of fresh because the flavor of the bottled lemon juice is inferior. I buy big bags full or lemons and limes! To squeeze them I have a handy little juicer. It is a standard juicing top that fits like a lid over the bowl that has a pouring spout in it. When I have juice leftover, I simply stick it in the refrigerator ready for next time.

Eggs. We go through SO many eggs! I have found a local pharmacy that sells them very inexpensively, otherwise I might need to get chickens!

Another item that I either need to figure out how to make, or I need to purchase stock in the company, is pork rinds. Yes, deep fried pig skins! I rarely actually eat them plain, but I use them constantly. I use them for a filler in meat balls, salmon patties and the like, I use them as a breading, I even use them in some desserts. When they are seasoned properly, I can't even tell they are pork rinds. I have a small well sealed container that I try to keep full of pre-ground pork rinds. It is usually empty! I grind up one or two bags at a time that way I won't have to do it every time I need them. That is the theory anyway.

SteviaPlus® and sucralose packets are the sweeteners I use. I find it simpler than using the liquid extracts. The measurements are more straight-forward.

I keep almonds on hand, both raw and blanched almonds. I use the raw ones as a portable snack that I keep in my purse for those occasions when there is simply NO food to eat! I also use them for making ground almonds, sometimes called almond flour. I just fill my food processor with what ever amount I need and chop away! I just have to be careful, if it is processed too long, the oils will separate out and it will be almond butter. Yummy, but doesn't work in place of the ground nuts. The same goes for any nut, simply grind it to the desired state – either flour or butter, depending on how long it is processed. When making the nut butter, mine always forms a ball. That is how I know when it is done. One note: For the best results in nut butter, be sure and have the hopper of the food processor at least half full. Otherwise the motor will have to work much harder. To just make the flour, it isn't necessary to have a full processor. Although, I do usually grind extra and put it in a tightly sealed container ready for future use.

I also keep salted sunflower seeds and macadamia flour (ground macadamias) on hand, but the almonds are essential because I use them as a base for my almond milk. I use it in place of the cream that most folks on this way of eating can have.

Certain spices and seasonings are pantry basics: Seasoning salt, lemon pepper, garlic salt, mustard powder, ground ginger, dried onions, dried parsley, dried chives, ground ginger, cinnamon, vanilla and almond extract. There are a lot of others that I use as well: Rosemary, lemon thyme, mint, fresh chives, fresh garlic and onions. The seasoning salt I use has no sugar in it and the lemon pepper I use doesn't have salt or sugar in it. It is just black pepper, lemon peel and lemon oil. I suppose I could make my own, but the lemon oil would be tricky! Besides, I get it in the bulk section of my local grocery and it is really inexpensive. I get the majority my herbs and seasoning that I don't grow myself in the bulk section.

Grated orange rind or lemon rind is also a nice thing to have and is a snap to make with a food processor. Just take the leftover peel, without the membranes, place it in the food processor with the chopping blade in place. Chop the peel until finely ground. Lay the chopped peel out on a baking sheet in an oven set at the lowest temperature for about 2 hours or until it looks well dried (a deep golden brown), but not scorched. It can also be left out to air-dry in some low-use area, (for me the top of the microwave), for a couple of days. No worries about over drying that way! Store in an airtight container.

Arrowroot powder is a handy thickening agent. It doesn't reheat very well in some foods, and needs to be used right away once it's been put in something, but it does produce a nice clear finish to foods. It is indispensable to me for soups and gravies. I buy it in bulk at my health food store and store it in an airtight container. Guar gum is another thickener. I do not prefer it for gravies, but it definitely has uses as a thickener. It is stable, where arrowroot breaks down, and can be used in either cold or hot foods. Arrowroot also has bio-available carbs where guar gum is pure fiber! From what I understand, it passes right through the body, unprocessed.

I keep soy protein (NOT soy flour!) on hand, for use in small amounts in baking. It can also be called soy powder, or several other things from what I understand. It is usually marketed as a meal replacement drink and can be found in that section of grocery stores. I use if for a flour substitute, and it has the consistency of cornstarch.

For the rest of my family I have granulated fructose, rolled oats, whole spelt and rye flours, but I don't use them, personally.

I always try to keep a cabbage in the refrigerator, as well as a bag of commercially pre-washed spinach leaves. The spinach keeps much longer that way, and the price is usually comparable in my area. Rutabagas, celery and cauliflower are nice to have, and so are radishes. Radishes are great for a quick veggie when I don't have time to cook something. I wash and trim them when I get them home from the store and keep them in an airtight container. They will stay nice for over a week that way. Handy for snacking or in salads. Generally, I try to buy what ever is in season and on sale. I am pretty adventurous with food and like to try new things. You'll often find me asking the produce man at the store questions about different things. The same is true for the meat and seafood departments. This love for trying new things has been passed onto my children. They thoroughly enjoy most of my experiments! In fact, most of our home school science experiments are based on food.

I try to keep canned or frozen green beans around because sometimes we do run out of fresh vegetables. (I always prefer fresh.) Along that same line, canned tuna, canned salmon and sardines are good things to have because they provide an easy source of protein. I eat the sardines on sliced zucchinis or cauliflower slices, and they can be eaten on cucumber slices and pork rinds as well. Canned olives are another staple at this house because they are quick and yummy.

The Rich Stock (broth) recipe (see recipe, p. 155) is something I always keep on hand, too. I freeze it in my ice cube trays and put the cubes in gallon zipper-sealed bags in my freezer. I use some of it almost ever day! I use it for marinating beef jerky, sauces, and re-heating foods to keep them from drying out.

THE RECIPES?

The recipes in the book are mostly candida friendly. That is how I cook! I have included a few non-candida friendly recipes, but they are all clearly marked with an "*" and the phrase "This recipe not suitable for candida sufferers." Also, whenever a non-candida friendly ingredient is included, I've indicated that by saying "not if you have candida" next to the ingredient listed.

What are non-candida friendly ingredients? Vinegar, cheese, all dairy, peanuts, pistachios, mushrooms, soy sauce, sugar, white flour and any other food that is high in carbohydrate content. Anything containing yeast or that can be turned into sugar in the body, like fruit, as well as anything fermented must be avoided. Sounds like a lot of food, doesn't it? It is! But, I have found there are a lot of other wonderful foods out there just waiting to be discovered, while getting my candida under control and losing weight. That is a happy combination!

What about the inability to use vinegar, soy sauce and sweetener? I use lemon in the place of vinegar, seasoning salt and lemon pepper and broth substitute for soy sauce, and I use SteviaPlus® and sucralose for sweeteners. What are SteviaPlus® and sucralose? Sucralose is a better alternative to aspartame, which has been rumored to cause dire health problems. I personally do not react adversely to aspartame, but it isn't heat stable. Sucralose is another artificial sweetener, but it is sugar based, so it has a nicer flavor. I try not to use too much of it though. I try to get the majority of the sweetness in my recipes from SteviaPlus®, just using the sucralose as a balance for the intensity of the SteviaPlus®. While aspartame is reported to be bad for you, and sucralose seems to be simply not bad for you; SteviaPlus® is an herbal sweetener that is actually good for you! It is reported to aid in digestion, which anyone with candida will be happy about! It is a very potent sweetener and needs to be used in small amounts. It is a white powder that is about 30 times sweeter than sugar. A little goes a long way! For specific questions about SteviaPlus®, they may be contacted at www.wisdomherbs.com.

As I alluded to earlier, I have also included a "regular" section in the back that simply has sugar-free recipes. They are NOT low carb or for candida sufferers. They were developed with my children in mind, mostly. As I said earlier, my son is allergic to sugar, so I've adapted some favorite recipes for his benefit. I don't allow him to eat vast quantities of these things. They are high in carb content, and that is not good for anyone at any age!

I've included carb counts with each of the recipes, excluding the sugar-free non-low carb section. Each recipe lists the carb count for the entire recipe, individual servings, fiber and ECC. What is ECC? ECC is an abbreviation for Effective Carb Count. Some low carb plans allow for the deduction of fiber from the total carbohydrate content of the food. For instance, if a recipe has 10 carbs, 5 of them being fiber, the ECC would be 5 carbs. That means the carbs that are bio-available, (able to be used by our bodies), are only 5 rather than the full 10 listed.

I hope you enjoy my recipes and get a lot of good use out of the information presented.

Blessings!

Breakfasts

1946 Pork Sausage

This is my sister's favorite sausage recipe. When she got married in 1969, she was given a set of cookbooks that were printed in 1946. She says they are her most-used cookbooks! The basic idea for this sausage came from those cookbooks.

4 pounds ground pork
1 teaspoon cayenne pepper
1 teaspoon salt
1 1/2 teaspoons lemon pepper
2 teaspoons ground sage

Combine all ingredients in a mixing bowl. Mix well. Form into patties, or crumble and cook in a frying pan until well done. Serves 4.

Negligible carbs.

This is just a simple "old time" sausage recipe. Good for folks who don't like the fancier sausages. If you like things HOT use up to 1 1/2 teaspoons cayenne.

Best Bacon

I'm sure you're wondering why I am putting cooking instructions for bacon in this cookbook. Aren't the directions right on the package? They are, but the package will never tell how to get picture perfect bacon every time. I learned this while I was working at a very nice retreat center in the Willamette Valley, Oregon.

1 pound bacon, cured without sugar

Lay bacon out evenly on a large baking sheet. Be sure edges don't overlap. All of the bacon may not fit on the baking sheet at first. The bacon will shrink as it cooks, leaving excess room. The additional slices may be added in at that time. Place baking sheet in 350° F oven for approximately 30 minutes. Remove when the fatty portion is translucent; it should no longer be white. It won't appear brown the way pan fried bacon does, but the meat will be a deep red color. If it is overcooked, it will crumble when cooled. If it is perfect, it will be tender and juicy. It will also lay out flat, rather than being curly and lumpy. Place on a serving plate lined with paper towels to drain. Serves 4.

No carbs.

Tip: Save the bacon grease in a jar with a lid, and you'll get some "free" cooking oil out of it! Just be sure to place a metal object into the jar before you pour the hot grease into it. Then pour the grease in so it touches the metal object first. Otherwise, the glass will explode from contact with the heat. This applies to any glass dish. Always put a metal spoon, knife, whatever, into the bottom of the dish before adding anything hot right from the stove or oven. You'll reduced the risk of injury as well as making your dishes last longer!

Breakfast Burritos

*This recipe is not suitable for candida sufferers

This is a staple at my house. Unfortunately, I am allergic to wheat, so I can't have the low carb tortillas. Instead, I use regular whole wheat or corn tortillas for my kids, and they eat these all the time. I think it is one of their favorite breakfasts!

4 commercially prepared low carb tortillas
4 eggs
Seasoning salt
1/2 tablespoon butter
4 slices (4 ounces) Monterey Jack cheese
4 slices cooked bacon

Optional:
Commercially prepared salsa (without sugar, of course!)
Sour cream
Chives

Quickly pass tortillas through running water and allow to rest approximately 3 minutes. Heat a large skillet over medium heat and place tortillas into skillet one at a time, warming on each side about 30 to 45 seconds. Remove to plates. Place cheese and bacon down the center of each tortilla. Meanwhile, combine eggs and seasoning salt to taste in a small bowl, mixing thoroughly. Melt butter in a medium skillet over medium heat. Pour eggs into skillet and allow to cook without stirring until bottom becomes opaque and solid enough to flip, about 1 1/2 minutes. Turn eggs over and cook until done. Cut into 4 equal pieces. Put one piece on each tortilla. Fold tortillas up at the bottom and then over on each side. Serve with optional ingredients at the table. Serves 4.

Carb count: Varies according to brand of tortilla and choice of fillings.

Chubby Pancakes

Pancakes always remind me of Sunday mornings when I was growing up. Now they can be low carb!

2 eggs
1/2 cup Almond Milk (see recipe, p. 145) or 1/4 cup cream
    thinned to 1/2 cup (but not if you have candida)
1/2 teaspoon vanilla
1/2 cup ground pork rinds
3 tablespoons ground almonds
2 tablespoons soy protein (NOT soy flour!)
1/8 teaspoon SteviaPlus ®
1 packet sucralose
1/2 teaspoon cinnamon
Cooking oil

Combine eggs, almond milk and vanilla in a mixing bowl. Mix thoroughly. In a separate bowl combine pork rinds, almond flour, stevia, sucralose and cinnamon. Add dry ingredients to wet ingredients, stirring well. Allow mixture to rest for a few minutes. If it is too thick, add a little more almond milk until desired consistency is reached.

Heat large frying pan. Add enough oil to the pan to cover the bottom. Pour batter into pan, pancake style. Brown on each side and serve hot with almond butter and Sugar Free Pancake Syrup (see recipe, p. 58). Serves 2.

Carb counts: Entire recipe, 8.43. Fiber, 1.59. ECC, 4.92.
Per serving, 4.21. Fiber, .79. ECC, 2.46.

Cinnamon Butter

This butter is so rich and satisfying. It is great when something that tastes great is so simple! Excellent served with Pumpkin Waffles(see recipe, p. 54)!

6 tablespoons butter, room temperature
1 teaspoon SteviaPlus®
10 packets sucralose
1 1/2 teaspoons cinnamon

Combine all ingredients in a small mixing bowl. With an electric mixer, whip butter on medium speed, about 2 minutes. Put into a serving dish and chill until ready to use. Serves 6.

Carb count: Entire recipe 8.79, Fiber, 1.86. ECC, 6.88. Per serving, 1.45. Fiber, .31. ECC, 1.14.

Personal note: Butter is one of those foods that my mother's doctor had her give up "for her health." She was over 50, had high cholesterol, high blood pressure and emphysema. She dearly missed her butter, but ate the butter substitutes, so she could be "healthier." That promise failed her, and her health continued to decline. She passed away when she was 67 from complete cardio-pulmonary failure. Now, I wish he'd told her to give up her candy and ice cream. If only we had known...

Deviled Eggs With Bacon

On this way of eating I have chosen, I often eat scrambled eggs ad-infinitum. One can only eat so many scrambled eggs! This recipe came about because I didn't feel like cooking, but I did have some hard boiled eggs already prepared. Just something for a change of pace for breakfast!!

2 hard boiled eggs
1 piece cooked bacon, (sugar-free), finely chopped
1 1/2 tablespoons Blender Mayonnaise (see recipe, p. 147) or
    commercially prepared (if you don't have candida)
1/8 teaspoon dry mustard powder
1/4 teaspoon dehydrated onion
1/2 teaspoon parsley
Dash lemon pepper

Halve the eggs and remove the yolks. Set the whites aside on plate. Place the yolks, bacon, mayonnaise, mustard, onion, parsley and lemon pepper in a small bowl. Combine thoroughly. Fill the hollows in the egg whites with the yolk mixture. Garnish with parsley if desired. Serves one.

Carb count: Entire recipe, 1.81. Fiber, .15. ECC, 1.66.

Easy Cheesy Breakfast Pizza*

*This recipe is not suitable for candida sufferers

This makes a great breakfast or lunch!

6 eggs
3/4 teaspoon Italian seasoning herb blend
1/4 teaspoon seasoning salt
Cooking oil

Toppings:
Black olives, sliced
Green onions, sliced
Mushrooms
Cooked crumbled bacon
Cooked salad shrimp
Sliced cooked meat, etc.

4 ounces Monterey Jack or Mozzarella Cheese, sliced or grated

In a mixing bowl, combine the eggs, Italian seasonings, and seasoning salt. Set aside.

Pour about 2 tablespoons cooking oil into a 10" skillet with a lid. Place over medium heat. When the skillet is hot, add the egg mixture. Once during the cooking process, lift the eggs and allow the excess uncooked eggs to flow under. When the eggs are nearly set, and there is no longer any excess uncooked egg, begin putting toppings of choice on egg crust. Spread them evenly so the surface area is well covered. Spread cheese over all. Cover and remove the pan from heat. Allow to rest about 3 minutes, or until the cheese is melted. Cut into wedges and serve. Serves 2 to 4 depending upon appetite! Carb count: Varies according to toppings used.

If multiplying this recipe, or if many toppings are used, it may be necessary to put the entire pan, uncovered, into the oven and broil for about 3 minutes for the cheese to melt properly.

Farmer's Breakfast

I was friends with a family that owned a farm during my college years. I have fond memories of bucking hay, picking asparagus and strawberries, and the wonderful food. The mother of the family made such delicious breakfasts! This recipe reminds me of that time in my life.

1 small sweet onion chopped fine
1/2 pound Sharron's Pork Sausage (see recipe, p. 56) or
      1946 Pork Sausage (see recipe, p. 39)
8 eggs
1 tablespoon parsley flakes
Seasoning salt
2 tablespoons bacon grease or other cooking oil
Low carb tortillas, for serving (optional)

In a medium skillet, over medium heat, cook the onion in the bacon grease until it is translucent, about 3 minutes. Add the sausage and heat through. In a mixing bowl, scramble the eggs, parsley and seasoning salt to taste. Pour the egg mixture over the sausage mixture in the skillet. Cook through, stirring frequently. Optional: Serve hot with warmed low carb tortillas for scooping. Serves 4.

Carb count: Entire recipe, 11. Fiber, 2.37. ECC, 8.63, not including the tortillas.
Per serving, 2.75. Fiber, .59. ECC, 2.16, not including the tortilla.

I'm Eating It So Fast Because It Is So Good (a One Skillet Meal)

What kind of a name it that? It is what my little son said when he started eating. He ate a lot!

1/3 cup fresh minced onion
2 cloves garlic, minced
2 tablespoons cooking oil
2 cups Baked Winter Squash (see recipe, p. 115), cut into 1/2"
    cubes
1/2 teaspoon seasoning salt
1/4 teaspoon lemon pepper
1 cup ham, cut into 1/2" cubes (sugar free, of course)
6 eggs
1/2 teaspoon seasoning salt (or to taste)
1/2 tablespoon parsley
3/4 cup Monterey Jack and/or cheddar cheese, cut into 1/2"
    cubes (but not if you have candida)

In a large skillet with a well fitting lid, place onion, garlic and cooking oil. Cook over medium heat until onions are becoming translucent, about 1 1/2 minutes. Add winter squash, seasoning salt and lemon pepper. Cook uncovered about 5 minutes, until the squash is becoming golden. Turn and cook another 3 to 5 minutes. Be careful not to overcook the squash at this stage. It should stay fairly firm and in cubes.

Meanwhile, in a medium bowl beat the eggs with the seasoning salt and parsley. Set aside. Add the ham to the squash mixture and heat through. Stir well and spread evenly over the bottom of skillet. Pour the egg mixture over all and cook, turning occasionally, until almost set. Drop the cheese cubes evenly over the surface of the egg mixture. Remove from heat and cover. Allow to rest about 5 minutes, or until cheese melts. Serves 4.

Carb count: Entire recipe, 47.52. Fiber, 12.73. ECC, 34.79.
Per serving, 11.88. Fiber, 3.19. ECC, 8.69.

Maple Pork Sausage

When my husband and I were first married, we were still in college. There was a little grocery store just down the street that made fresh sausage in their meat department. My favorite was their maple pork sausage. This recipe was inspired by that sausage.

1 1/4 pounds ground pork
1/2 teaspoon maple extract
1 teaspoon fennel/anise seed
1 teaspoon seasoning salt
1 teaspoon minced dried onion
1/4 teaspoon lemon pepper
1/2 teaspoon dried sage
Pinch SteviaPlus® OR 1/2 packet sucralose
3 drops hot chili oil or a tiny pinch of cayenne

Place all the ingredients into a deep mixing bowl and combine thoroughly. This sausage may be made into patties or just cooked and crumbled to be added to eggs, casseroles, etc... Serves 6 with negligble carbs.

Excellent served alongside Chubby Pancakes (see recipe, p. 42) with Sugar Free Pancake Syrup (see recipe, p. 58)!

Note: Any of the sausage recipes in this book may be made by substituting ground beef, ground chicken or ground turkey for the ground pork.

Omelettes With or Without Cheese

For the longest time I thought I couldn't have omelettes because I couldn't have cheese. Then one day, the light dawned: I don't need to have cheese to have a yummy omelette! Eat 'em up, they are yummy and, oh, so good for you!

3 eggs
1/2 teaspoon parsley flakes
1/2 teaspoon dried chives
Seasoning salt to taste
1/2 tablespoon butter, bacon grease or other cooking oil

Filling ingredients (choose one or several!):
2 ounces cheese (Monterey Jack, Colby, Swiss, Cheddar, etc.)
      But not if you have candida
Chopped cooked bacon
Cooked shrimp meat
Cooked turkey, chicken or pork
Cooked zucchini, celery, peppers, onions, asparagus, mushrooms
      (not if you have candida), etc.
Cooked crumbled sausage

In a small bowl beat the eggs with seasoning salt, chives and parsley until very well combined. Heat cooking oil in a small skillet over medium heat until hot. Pour the eggs into the skillet, and cook until set. As the eggs are cooking, lift the edges so the uncooked portions will run under the cooked part. Cover half of the cooked eggs with your choices of meats and veggies.

Load it up! I especially like bacon and shrimp

Fold the empty half over the full half and slide onto a plate. Serves one.

Carb count: Varies according to choices made.

Parsley Eggs with Walla Walla Sweet Sauce

When I was a child growing up, I lived in Eastern Washington State. Those hot, arid conditions are perfect for growing big, sweet Walla Walla Sweet onions. My parents always got excited when Walla Walla Sweet season was upon us. Yearly, we drove over an hour into the hot country-side near Walla Walla, Washington, to find a roadside vendor. Every year, they bought a huge 20 pound bag of onions. We ate them in everything imaginable! I even remember my parents just peeling them and eating them like apples! Now that I'm an adult, I find myself getting excited about Walla Walla Sweet season, only I don't buy 20 pound bags of them! I do find them working their way into everything I cook, though. I will certainly be sad when they are unavailable again.

Sauce:
1 medium Walla Walla Sweet onion (or other sweet onion)
2 tablespoons bacon grease (or canola oil)
1 tablespoon butter
1/4 teaspoon garlic salt
1/8 teaspoon lemon pepper
1/2 tablespoon parsley
1/8 teaspoon seasoning salt
1/2 teaspoon arrowroot powder mixed into 1/4 cup water

Eggs:
8 eggs
1/2 teaspoon seasoning salt
1/2 teaspoon chives
1/2 teaspoon parsley
1 tablespoon cooking oil (canola preferred)

Slice the onion. In a medium skillet, over medium heat, cook the onion slice in bacon grease and butter. Add garlic salt, lemon pepper, parsley and seasoning salt. Continue cooking until the onion slices become translucent and begin to brown slightly. Add the arrowroot/water mixture and continue to cook and stir about one minute. Place in a small serving bowl.

In a mixing bowl, combine the eggs, seasoning salt, chives and parsley. Mix well. In a medium skillet over medium heat, heat cooking oil until hot. Pour the eggs into the skillet and cook through. When the eggs are no longer runny, remove to a serving dish.

Tip: When I need to put hot food into a cold glass or ceramic dish, I always put a metal spoon in the bowl first. As the hot food is poured into the dish, the metal spoon will absorb that first shock of heat and keep the glass from shattering.

To serve, place the desired amount of eggs on individual plates and spoon the sauce over the eggs. Serves 4.

Carb count: Eggs entire recipe, 5.01. Fiber, .07. ECC, 4.94.
Eggs per serving, 1.25. Fiber, .01. ECC, 1.23.
Sauce entire recipe, 11.24. Fiber, 2.24. ECC, 9.
Sauce per serving, 2.81. Fiber, .56. ECC, 2.25.

Pumpkin Spice Muffins

We lived in Dallas, Texas, during the first several years after our oldest child was born. It was there that I learned a lot about frugal living. Our finances had always been tight before that, but living on a single income, having a child and buying a house seemed to make things even tighter. I had a dear friend who loaned me periodicals about "tightwad" living. I spent many, many hours studying and taking notes. I learned about re-using plastic bags, duct taping broken laundry baskets and the author even wrote about dumpster-diving! It was at that point that I gave up reading those periodicals — dumpster-diving had pushed the limits of frugality just too far for me! While almost all of the "principles" I gleaned from that time in my life have gone by the wayside, one very useful things I did learn, and continue to use, was a great muffin recipe. Over the years I have adapted it and made it my own. Now, I have applied those principles and have low carbed it!

3/4 cup ground almonds
1/2 cup soy protein (NOT soy flour!)
1/2 teaspoon SteviaPlus®
4 packets sucralose
1 1/2 teaspoons baking powder
1/4 teaspoon salt
1 1/4 teaspoons pumpkin pie spice (or 1 teaspoon cinnamon
     and 1/4 teaspoon nutmeg)
1/2 cup pecan or walnut meats, broken into 1/4" to 1/2" pieces
1/2 cup Almond Milk (see recipe, p. 145) or 1/4 cup cream
     thinned to 1/2 cup (but not if you have candida)
2 tablespoons cooking oil (olive preferred)
1 egg
1/2 cup pumpkin puree
Cooking oil spray

Topping:

6 tablespoons ground almonds
3 tablespoons butter
1/2 teaspoon SteviaPlus® or 2 packets sucralose
1/2 teaspoon cinnamon

In a large mixing bowl, combine the ground almonds, soy protein, SteviaPlus®, sucralose, baking powder, salt, pumpkin pie spice and nut meats. Mix well and set aside. In a small mixing bowl, combine the Almond Milk, cooking oil, egg and pumpkin. Mix thoroughly, until uniform in texture. Add the wet ingredients all at once to the dry ingredients, mixing until just combined. The batter should be slightly lumpy. Spray a standard size muffin tin with cooking oil spray. Place the batter in the muffin cups so that they are about 2/3 full.

If any muffins cups remain empty, place about 1 tablespoon water in each cup. This keeps the muffins moist and prevents the pan from burning.

Using a food processor with a chopping blade or a pastry blender, combine topping ingredients. The topping will be sticky. Press the topping evenly over the muffins. Bake at 400° F for 15 minutes, or until a toothpick inserted in the center comes out clean. Allow muffins to rest one minute, then remove by sliding a table knife around the edge of each muffin. Place muffins on a cooling rack and allow to rest about 5 minutes. Serve warm with butter. Makes 8.

Carb count: Entire recipe, 51.97. Fiber, 26.15. ECC, 25.82. Per serving, 6.49. Fiber, 3.26. ECC, 3.22.

Pumpkin Waffles

My husband grew up kid in the tropical jungles of Ecuador. Needless to say, it was an incredible growing up experience! Whenever he talks about Ecuador, or sees a special on television, he gets this far-away look on his face. One of the foods my husband talks of with special fondness is waffles. Unfortunately, I have never been much of a waffle baker. I didn't even get a waffle iron until we had been married about 6 or 7 years! Thankfully, food has never held much power over him, and he has always enjoyed what I fixed for him, (well, most of the time! No one is perfect!). He learned to like the foods I cook for him, but whenever waffles are even mentioned, he gets that far-away look in his eyes. I hope you enjoy these waffles as much as my family does. They are perfect for special breakfasts, and Sunday evening waffles. And, yes, my husband does get that far-away look when he eats them!

1/3 cup blanched almonds
1 1/2 cups water
3 eggs, beaten
1/2 cup pumpkin
2 tablespoons butter, melted
2/3 cup ground pork rinds
2 tablespoons soy protein (NOT soy flour!)
1/4 cup ground almonds
2 teaspoons baking powder
2 packets sucralose
1/8 teaspoon SteviaPlus®
1/4 teaspoon pumpkin pie spice (or 1/8 teaspoon each
     cinnamon and nutmeg)

If almonds are not pre-blanched, place them in a bowl, pour

in enough water to cover and microwave for about 2 minutes. The skins should become loose and peel easily. Remove and discard skins. Place blanched almonds in blender container and discard blanching water. Add water.

I always use filtered water in all my cooking! That way the taste of chlorine and other chemicals doesn't interfere with the taste of the food.

Blend, beginning on low then turning up to high, until almonds are completely pulverized, about 1 1/2 to 2 minutes. Set aside.

In a large mixing bowl, combine eggs and pumpkin. Stir in the pulverized almond/water mixture and butter.

In a small bowl combine the pork rinds, soy protein, ground almonds, baking powder, sucralose, SteviaPlus ® and pumpkin pie spice. Stir dry ingredients into wet until just combined. Allow the batter to rest at least 5 minutes before baking on a hot, greased waffle iron. Bake waffles until steam disappears and waffles are golden brown, about 10 minutes each. Makes 4 - 8" waffles.

Theses are excellent served with Cinnamon Butter (see recipe, p. 43) and Vanilla Sauce (see recipe, p. 59)!

Carb count: Entire recipe, 29.45. Fiber, 12.02. ECC, 17.41. Per serving, 7.36. Fiber, 3.0. ECC, 4.35.

Shannon's Pork Sausage

I like to crumble sausage and pre-cook it. Then I place it on a baking sheet sprayed with cooking spray and freeze it in my chest freezer. When it's frozen, I store it in freezer bags for a pre-cooked addition to recipes. I also make uncooked pre-formed patties in the same manner. After I've shaped them and frozen them, the patties can then be stored in freezer bags like the cooked variation. Makes breakfast on busy mornings so much easier!

2 pounds ground pork
2 cloves fresh minced garlic (OR 1/2 teaspoon garlic granules, but fresh is always best!)
1/2 to 1 teaspoon fennel or anise seed (some like less, I like more!)
1 teaspoon seasoning salt
1 tablespoon minced dried onion
1/2 teaspoon lemon pepper
1/2 teaspoon dried sage
1/4 teaspoon SteviaPlus ® or 1/2 packet sucralose
1/2 teaspoon hot chili oil or a pinch of cayenne
1/4 teaspoon thyme
1/4 teaspoon marjoram

Place all the ingredients into a deep mixing bowl and combine thoroughly. This may be made into patties or just cooked and crumbled to be added to eggs, casseroles, etc... Serves 8.

Carb count: Entire recipe, 8.2. Fiber, 1.86. ECC, 6.61.
Per serving, 1.02. Fiber, .23. ECC, .82.

Variations:
Italian Sausage: Add 1/2 tablespoon Italian Seasonings to the above.

Spicy Sausage: Add 1/2 teaspoon red pepper flakes and double the sage and lemon pepper.

Spinach Quiche

There are so many variations on quiche. This is one my family particularly enjoys!

1/3 cup onion, chopped
1/2 tablespoon butter
1 cup spinach, raw
4 eggs
1/2 teaspoon seasoning salt
Pinch of nutmeg (ever so much less than 1/8 teaspoon!)
1/2 tablespoon dried parsley
5 drops hot chili oil (Yes, DROPS!)
2 cups Almond Milk (see recipe, p. 145) or 2 cups cream (but not if you have candida!)
5 pieces cooked bacon
Cooking oil spray

Optional:
1/2 cup shredded Swiss or Monterey jack cheese (but not if you have candida!)

In a small frying pan melt the butter over medium heat. Add the onions and cook until translucent, about 3 minutes. Set aside and allow to cool. Chop the spinach, and set aside. In a large mixing bowl, using a wire whisk or fork, beat eggs. Add the cooled onions, seasoning salt, nutmeg, parsley, hot chili oil, Almond Milk and spinach, mixing thoroughly. Spray a 9" or 10" pie plate with cooking oil spray. Cut the bacon up into 1/2" pieces and lay evenly in pie plate. Add the cheese and pour the egg/milk mixture carefully over all. Bake 375° F for 40 minutes or until a knife inserted off center comes out clean. Cool 10 minutes. I prefer this served hot, although it may also be served warm or cold. Serves 4.

Carb count: Entire recipe, 15.67. Fiber, 3.21. ECC, 12.46. Per serving, 3.91. Fiber, .8. ECC, 3.11.

Variation: Broccoli Quiche – Substitute 1 cup chopped, cooked broccoli for the spinach. Follow all directions as given.

Sugar Free Pancake Syrup

We have to have syrup for our pancakes, don't we?

1/2 teaspoon imitation maple flavoring
8 packets sucralose
1/2 tablespoon SteviaPlus®
1 cup water
2 teaspoons arrowroot powder (OR 1/4 teaspoon guar gum)
    mixed into 1/4 cup water

Combine the maple flavoring, sucralose, SteviaPlus®, and 1 cup water in a small sauce pan. Heat until boiling. Pour the arrowroot/water mixture into the boiling syrup. Stir until thickened.

Arrowroot produces lovely sauces, but does require some care. It is very delicate and doesn't like to be stirred too much. Be sure and mix the arrowroot into cold water, not right into the hot liquid. If you mix it into the hot liquid, you will end up with a little gelatin ball! Pour the arrowroot/water mixture into the boiling liquid and stir it until just combined. Remove it from the heat as soon as it thickens, otherwise it begins to break down quickly. I believe it is well worth the effort for the results!

Remove from heat and serve warm over Chubby Pancakes (see recipe, p. 42) or Wonderful Waffles (see recipe, p. 60). Serves 4.

Carb count for entire recipe made with arrowroot, 2.93. Negligible carb count per individual serving.

I much prefer the flavor of the syrup made with the arrowroot over that made with the guar gum.

Vanilla Sauce

On the morning I came up with this recipe, I had some of the sauce leftover. I wasn't sure what to do with it — whether I should save it or not — so I left it on the dining table for a little while. While I was trying to decide what to do with it, my children came along and saw it sitting there. Within about two minutes it was gone. No more decision to make!

1 cup water
1/4 teaspoon SteviaPlus®
3 packets sucralose
1/2 tablespoon arrowroot mixed into 1/4 cup water
3 tablespoons butter
2 teaspoons vanilla

Bring the water to a boil in a small saucepan. Sprinkle the SteviaPlus® and sucralose over the boiling water and stir until combined. Pour in the arrowroot/water and stir until thickened and fairly clear. Remove from heat and add the butter and vanilla, stirring until the butter melts. Serve warm. Serves 6.

Wonderful with Pumpkin Waffles (see recipe, p. 54) and Cinnamon Butter (see recipe, p. 43)!

Carb count: Entire recipe, 6.38. Fiber, .13. ECC, 6.25. Per serving, 1.06. Fiber, .02. ECC, 1.04.

Wonderful Waffles

Fall mornings, lazy Saturdays... Those are the perfect time for Wonderful Waffles!

1 cup Almond Milk (see recipe, p. 145) or 1/2 cup cream thinned to 1 cup (but not if you have candida)
1 teaspoon vanilla
2 eggs, separated
3 tablespoons canola oil
1 cup ground pork rinds
2 tablespoons soy protein (NOT soy flour!)
1/4 cup ground almonds
1 teaspoon baking powder
1/2 teaspoon SteviaPlus®
2 packets sucralose
1 1/2 teaspoons cinnamon

In a large mixing bowl, combine the Almond Milk, vanilla, egg yolks and canola oil. Set aside. In a small bowl, combine the pork rinds, soy protein, ground almonds, baking powder, SteviaPlus®, sucralose and cinnamon. Stir the dry ingredients into the wet ingredients until just combined.

In a small bowl with an electric mixer, whip the egg whites until stiff peaks form. Fold the beaten egg whites into the batter until just combined. There should still be a few egg white "puffs" left visible. Allow the batter to rest while waffle iron heats up. Bake on a well greased, hot waffle iron until they stop steaming and are golden brown. Serve hot. Makes 3 - 8" waffles.

Serve with Sugar-Free Pancake Syrup (see recipe, p. 58)!

Carb count: Entire recipe, 14.02. Fiber, 6.83. ECC, 7.19. Per serving, 4.67. Fiber, 2.27. ECC, 2.4.

Zucchini Nut Muffins

Late summer and zucchinis are synonymous. Some of my earliest "foody" memories were of my mother, bless her heart, gathering tomatoes, bell peppers and zucchinis fresh from the garden. She brought them in and lovingly prepare them into "stewed tomatoes." Eeeewww!! I never was able to get past that first bite. Way too yucky for this little girl! I found out later that I am terribly allergic to both tomatoes and bell peppers. I am not allergic to zucchini, though, and I have found many wonderful things to do with this sometimes dainty, often huge, late summer veggie. These delicious muffins are just one example. Enjoy!

3/4 cup ground almonds
1/2 cup soy protein (NOT soy flour!)
1/2 teaspoon SteviaPlus®
4 packets sucralose
1 1/2 teaspoons baking powder
1/4 teaspoon salt
1/2 teaspoon cinnamon
1/4 teaspoon nutmeg
1/2 teaspoon orange or lemon zest
1/2 cup pecan or walnut meats, broken into 1/4" to 1/2" pieces
1/2 cup Almond Milk (see recipe, p. 147) or 1/4 cup cream
      thinned to 1/2 cup (but not if you have candida)
2 tablespoons cooking oil (olive preferred)
1 egg
1/2 cup shredded zucchini
Cooking oil spray

Topping:
6 tablespoons ground almonds
3 tablespoons butter
1/2 teaspoon SteviaPlus® or 2 packets sucralose
1/4 teaspoon orange or lemon zest
1/4 teaspoon cinnamon

In a large mixing bowl, combine the ground almonds, soy protein, stevia, sucralose, baking powder, salt, cinnamon, nutmeg, lemon zest and nut meats. Mix well and set aside.

In a small mixing bowl, combine the Almond Milk, cooking oil, egg and zucchini. Mix thoroughly, until uniform in texture. Add the wet ingredients all at once to the dry ingredients, mixing until just combined. The batter should be slightly lumpy.

Spray a standard size muffin tin with cooking oil spray. Place the batter in muffin cups so that they are about 2/3 full.

If any muffins cups remain empty, place about 1 tablespoon water in each cup. This keeps the muffins moist and prevents the pan from burning.

Using a food processor with a chopping blade or a pastry blender, combine the topping ingredients. Press evenly over muffins. Bake at 400° F for 15 minutes, or until a toothpick inserted in the center comes out clean. Allow the muffins to rest one minute, then remove them from the pan and place on a cooling rack. Serve warm with butter. Makes 8.

Carb count: Entire recipe, 54.68. Fiber, 32.69. ECC, 21.99. Per serving, 6.84. Fiber, 4.09. ECC, 2.75.

Main Courses

Baked Fish Macadamia

This is by far the best fish I have ever made! It was just incredible....

4 large pieces pollock or other white fish suitable for breading
2 eggs
2 tablespoons water
1/3 pound ground macadamia nuts
Seasoning salt
Lemon pepper
3 tablespoons cooking oil (canola preferred)
Cooking oil spray
Lemon juice for serving at table

Pour approximately 2-3 tablespoons cooking oil into an 11″ by 17″ baking pan.

In a shallow dish, beat the eggs and water. In another small shallow dish, place some of the ground macadamia nuts and season to taste with seasoning salt. Prepare the ground macadamia nuts in small batches or it will become too sticky and you'll waste it. Only prepare enough for 2-3 pieces of fish at a time.

Cut fish into serving size pieces about 3″ to 4″ long. Dip the pieces in the egg mixture then roll in the macadamia mixture. This part of the process is very messy! Gently place the fish in the baking pan about 1″ to 2″ apart. When done, sprinkle the tops of the fish with lemon pepper and spray with cooking oil spray, to aid in browning. Bake at 375° F approximately 15 to 20 minutes, until macadamia topping is lightly browned. To serve, squeeze fresh lemon on top. Serves 4 adults.

Carb count: Entire recipe, 22.09. Fiber, 11.97. ECC, 10.12. Per serving, 5.52. Fiber, 2.99. ECC, 2.53.

Barbecue Chicken

We had some friends over for dinner and had been discussing this book earlier in the evening. When they were leaving, she said, "You are going to put the chicken in the book, aren't you?" I replied, "Well, no, it's just barbecue chicken..." Then she told me, "But the flavor was just fabulous! You've got to put it in there!" Here it is.

1 whole frying chicken cut-up, or the equivalent in pieces
Lemon pepper
Seasoning salt
Mesquite charcoal briquettes or chips

Season both sides of the meat liberally with seasoning salt and lemon pepper. Using a barbecue with a cover, place the meat on the highest rack setting (about 5" to 6" away from coals) over medium-hot coals. Cover the barbecue and allow the meat to smoke, turning it occasionally. Cook it for about 45 minutes or until the meat is golden brown and firm to the touch. Serve hot. Serves 4.

Using the meat thermometer is discouraged when barbecuing because those precious juices are lost!

No carbs.

Barbecue Pork

I've always wondered how they get that red edging on the meat at Asian restaurants. I just figured it was because of some sort of sauce or food dye. Nope, it is just the effect of the smoking process!

4 boneless pork loin chops or ribs
Seasoning salt
Lemon pepper
Mesquite charcoal briquettes or chips

Season both sides of the meat liberally with seasoning salt and lemon pepper. Using a barbecue with a cover, place the meat on the highest rack setting (about 5″ to 6″ away from coals) over medium-hot coals. Cover the barbecue and allow the meat to smoke, turning it occasionally. Cook it for about 30 minutes. The meat should have a deep reddish appearance and be firm to the touch when done.

Using the meat thermometer is discouraged when barbecuing because those precious juices are lost!

Remove from heat and slice thinly. Serve hot with sauces of choice. Offer sesame seeds alongside the sauces for dipping. Serves 4 with no carbs.

Serve alongside Egg Rolls (see recipe, p. 126) or Sesame Slaw (see recipe, p. 159) for an Asian-style meal!

Note: Save the leftovers and use for either Fried Rice-aflower (see recipe, p. 78) or "Ham" Salad (see recipe, p. 80)

Beef Gravy Supreme

Serve this over Baked Spaghetti Squash (see recipe, p. 115) for a yummy dinner!

1/2 large sweet onion, chopped
1 tablespoon cooking oil (canola preferred)
2 pounds ground beef
2 stalks celery, chopped
4 cloves fresh garlic, minced (or 1/2 teaspoon garlic salt and omit salt/lite salt)
2 tablespoons fresh parsley, chopped (or 1 tablespoon dried)
1 mint leaf (1/2 teaspoon, approximately), chopped (or 1/2 teaspoon of mint from an unused mint tea bag would work)
1/2 teaspoon fresh lemon thyme, chopped (or 1/4 teaspoon dried thyme would work if no lemon thyme is available)
1/2 teaspoon lemon pepper
1/8 teaspoon dry mustard powder
1 teaspoon seasoning salt
1/8 teaspoon SteviaPlus® or 1/2 packet sucralose
1/8 hot chili oil or a few grains of cayenne
1 1/2 cups water OR Beef or Pork Rich Stock (see recipe, p. 155)
1 tablespoon arrowroot mixed into 1/2 cup water

In a small skillet cook the onion in the oil until translucent and it begins to brown around the edges. Meanwhile, in a large skillet with a lid, brown the ground beef. Add the cooked onions with their juices. Stir in the celery, garlic, parsley, mint, lemon thyme, lemon pepper, salt, mustard, seasoning salt, SteviaPlus®, chili oil and water or stock. Cover and simmer 45 minutes to 1 hour. Add the arrowroot/water mixture to the boiling gravy and stir. Serves 6.

Variation:
Beef Stroganoff Supreme: Add 1/2 cup dairy sour cream or whole milk yogurt just before serving, but not if you have candida.

Carb count: Entire recipe, 20.42. Fiber, 3.66. ECC, 16.75
Per serving, 3.4. Fiber, .61. ECC, 2.79.

Beef Stew With Pumpkin

Super hearty! Warm and satisfying for those cold winter nights.

2 pounds beef stew meat
2 tablespoons cooking oil (canola preferred)
1/2 teaspoon seasoning salt
1 medium sweet onion, chopped
1 clove elephant garlic or 2 cloves garlic, minced
2 bay leaves
4" tops from one bunch celery OR 2 large stalks celery, chopped
2 small turnips, cut into 3/4" cubes
2 carrots, cut into 1/2" chunks (optional)
1/2 head cabbage, cut into 1 1/2" cubes
1/2 teaspoon seasoning salt
1/4 teaspoon basil
1/4 lemon pepper
1 cup pumpkin puree

Place the stew meat and cooking oil in a 5 quart stock pot. Season with 1/2 teaspoon seasoning salt. Cook over medium heat until the meat loses most of its redness, about 5 minutes. Add the onion and garlic, and continue to cook until the onion is translucent, about 3 to 4 minutes. Add the bay leaves, celery, turnips, (carrots), cabbage, 1/2 teaspoon seasoning salt, basil, and lemon pepper. Cover tightly and allow to simmer on low 4 to 6 hours. After that time, remove the bay leaves and add the pumpkin to the pot. Simmer uncovered 5 minutes. Serves 6.

Note: There is no additional cooking liquid added to this recipe. It is very important to have a tightly fitting lid for your pan! Also, avoid opening the pan until after at least the first hour, or you will lose too much of the precious steam.

Carb count: Entire recipe, 68.17. Fiber, 23.98. ECC, 44.29.
Per serving, 11.36. Fiber, 3.99. ECC, 7.38.

Bonfire Barbecue Steak

We had a large bon-fire with some family friends. It was HUMONGOUS – nearly 12 feet across! The food turned out great!

1 1/2 pounds boneless London broil, or other boneless beef steak
    suitable for broiling
4 large cloves garlic
1/2 teaspoon seasoning salt
1/4 teaspoon lemon pepper
Foil
Large bon-fire, or other outdoor cooking fire

Before building your bonfire, slice the beef into 1/4" thick pieces, and place it into a container with a lid. Mince the garlic and stir it into the beef along with the seasoning salt and lemon pepper. Cover and allow the meat to rest while building the fire. When the coals are red-hot, it's time to do the cooking! Place 2 large sheets of foil crosswise, one on top of the other. Lay the meat out as thinly as possible across the wide middle part of the foil. Wrap it up tightly, pressing out any air and making sure there are no gaps in the wrapping. If necessary, place another sheet of foil around the meat. Place the meat bundle into the hot coals, and allow it to cook approximately 45 minutes, turning once part way through. Using a shovel or some other implement, remove the meat bundle from the fire. Allow the meat to rest 5 minutes. Carefully open the bundle, allowing the steam to escape. Serve hot with Roasted Veggies Over a Bonfire (see recipe, p. 134). Serves 4 with no carbs.

Hint: To remove the skin easily from a clove of fresh garlic, lay it on a cutting board and place the flat blade of a butcher knife across it. Give it a good thump with your fist, and then pick it up. The skin should virtually fall off, and the garlic is ready for mincing!

Chicken and Broccoli Alfredo*

*This recipe is not suitable for candida sufferers

1 whole chicken, cut up or 2 large breast pieces, cut up (about 3 1/2 pounds total either way)
1 bunch broccoli (about 1 1/2 pounds), cut up into 1 1/2" chunks
2 tablespoons butter
3 cloves garlic, minced
1 1/2 cups whipping cream
1 1/2 teaspoons arrowroot powder mixed into 1/4 cup water
1/2 cup Parmesan cheese
Salt and pepper to taste
Nutmeg for garnish, if desired

Place the chicken in a large baking dish and season with salt and pepper. Bake at 375° F for 50 to 60 minutes, or until the juices run clear. (About 40 minutes for breasts.)

Place the broccoli into a pot with about 1/2" of water. Cover the pan tightly and simmer the broccoli for about 10 minutes, or until it is tender.

Meanwhile, make the sauce by cooking the garlic in the butter over medium-low heat in a small sauce pan until garlic is translucent, about 3 minutes. Add the whipping cream and heat it until it is steaming. Add the arrowroot/water mixture, cooking until thickened. Remove it from the heat and add the Parmesan cheese, stirring to combine well. Add salt and pepper to taste.

Place the chicken pieces in a large serving bowl. Drain the broccoli and add it to the chicken in the serving bowl. Pour the sauce over the chicken and broccoli. Garnish with a light sprinkling of nutmeg, if desired. Serves 4.

Carb count: Entire recipe, 27.14. Fiber, 5.6. ECC, 21.54.
Per Serving, 6.79. Fiber, 1.4. ECC, 5.39.

Variation:
Broccoli Alfredo: Omit the chicken and simply use the broccoli and Alfredo sauce for a yummy side dish.

Chunky Beef Soup

Sometimes you just need a warm, satisfying, homemade soup. This is a good choice!

1 1/2 pounds beef stew meat
2 tablespoons cooking oil (canola preferred)
1 onion, cut into 3/4" cubes
4 cloves garlic, minced
1 carrot, cut into 1/2" cubes (optional)
1 small turnip, cut into 3/4" cubes
1 1/2 cups cabbage, cut into 3/4" cubes
1 bay leaf
1 1/2 teaspoons fresh lemon-thyme, minced*
2 tablespoons parsley, minced
2 cups water
1 teaspoon salt
1/2 teaspoon seasoning salt
1/4 teaspoon lemon pepper

In a large pot, place the cooking oil, meat, onion and garlic. Cook over medium heat, stirring often, until the meat begins to brown and the onion becomes translucent. Add the remaining ingredients. Cover and simmer for 1 hour. Some of the vegetables will have dissolved by this time, but it gives it a very rich broth, not needing any thickener. Remove the bay leaf and serve hot in bowls. Makes 4 servings.

*I suppose dried thyme could be used instead of the fresh, but it gave a wonderful fresh flavor to the soup!

Carb count: Entire recipe, 22.31. Fiber, 8.53. ECC, 13.78.
Per serving, 5.58. Fiber, 2.13. ECC, 3.45.

Clam Chowder

Do you ever wonder, "What can I do with those leftover broccoli and cauliflower stems?" Here's one option!

3 tablespoons butter
2 cloves garlic, minced
1/2 cup chopped sweet onion
1 cup peeled, cubed broccoli and/or cauliflower stem (or chopped cabbage, celery or cauliflower) cut into 1/4" to 1/2" pieces
1 1/2 cups stock: Either clam broth, (if it doesn't have any sugar), or Rich Chicken, Turkey or Pork Stock (see recipe, p. 155)
1/2 pound fresh or frozen chopped clams with juices (or equivalent canned if they don't have sugar)
1/4 teaspoon celery seed
1/2 teaspoon salt
1 teaspoon lemon pepper
4 drops hot chili oil, or a tiny pinch of cayenne
2 teaspoons arrowroot powder mixed into 1/4 cup water
2 pieces chopped cooked bacon without sugar (optional)
1 cup Almond Milk, unflavored (see recipe, p. 145) or cream (but not if you have candida)

In a medium sized sauce pan, melt the butter over medium-low heat. Add the garlic and onion and cook until translucent, about 3 to 5 minutes. Add the cubed broccoli and/or cauliflower, stock, clams, celery seed, salt, lemon pepper and chili oil. Cover and cook until the veggies are tender, about 10 minutes. Add the arrowroot/water mixture and bacon (optional). Simmer, stirring lightly until thickened. Add the almond milk and serve immediately. Makes about 4 one cup servings.

This doesn't get super thick like the commercial types of clam chowder, but it has a wonderful flavor.

Carb count: Entire recipe, 24.83. Fiber, 4.38. ECC, 20.45.
Per serving, 6.21. Fiber, 1.1. ECC, 5.11.

Corned Beef with Vegetables

It doesn't have to be St. Patrick's Day to enjoy a good corned beef!

2 1/2 pound fresh corned beef with seasoning herb packet
3 carrots, peeled and cut into 2" chunks (for non-low carbers)
3 large stalks celery, cut into 3" chunks
1 large sweet onion, sliced
4 cloves garlic, chopped
1/4 teaspoon seasoning salt
2 tablespoons cooking oil (canola preferred)
Water
1/3 head cabbage

Place the beef, herb packet, carrots and celery in 5 quart stock pot with a lid. In a small frying pan, cook the onion and garlic in the oil with the seasoning salt over medium heat. When the onions are translucent and becoming golden, add them to the beef and veggies. Add enough water to completely cover the beef. Bring it to a boil, cover and simmer 2 hours. During the cooking time, skim off any of the impurities that come to the top as foam and discard. When the 2 hours has just about passed, cut cabbage into wedges about 5" long and 2" wide. Place into the simmering pot, cover and cook 15 minutes. Continue to remove any impurities as they float to the top. Place the meat and veggies onto a large serving platter. Slice the meat thinly and serve with Honey Mustard Dipping Sauce (see recipe, p. 153) or Fiery Hot Mustard (see recipe, p. 150), if desired. Serves 4.

Carb count: Entire recipe, 63.08. Fiber, 19.75. ECC, 43.33
Entire recipe without carrots, 41.18. Fiber, 13.27. ECC, 27.91.
Per serving, 15.77. Fiber, 4.94. ECC, 10.83.
Per serving without carrots, 10.29. Fiber, 3.31. ECC, 6.97.

Cream of Leftover Soup

This is incredibly versatile! Makes a great lunch on a cold, rainy day!

1 to 1 1/2 pounds cooked meat, cut into 1" cubes (beef, pork, chicken, meatloaf, whatever!)
1 to 2 cups leftover cooked vegetables, diced (I happened to have 1 1/4 cups green beans on the day I did this)
1 small carrot, diced
1 cup finely chopped cauliflower
1/2 medium sized sweet onion, diced
2 cloves garlic, minced
2 stalks celery, or the leafy tops from one bunch, chopped
1 tablespoon parsley
1 teaspoon salt/lite salt
1/2 teaspoon lemon pepper
1/8 teaspoon basil
1/8 teaspoon celery seed
3 cups Rich Stock (see recipe, p. 155) -- beef, chicken or turkey, depending on what meat was chosen, or commercially prepared (if you don't have candida)
1/2 cup blanched almonds
2 cups water (OR instead of almonds/water, 1 cup cream plus an additional cup of Rich Stock may be substituted, if you don't have candida)
1 tablespoon butter

Place the meat, vegetables and seasonings into a 5 quart sauce pan with a lid. Pour the stock over all. Cover and bring it to a boil over medium heat. Reduce the heat and simmer for 30 minutes or until vegetables are tender. Meanwhile, place the water and almonds into a blender container and blend on high for approximately 1 1/2 minutes, or until the almonds are completely pulverized and the mixture is smooth. Pour it into the soup. Add the butter. Simmer uncovered 5 minutes. Serve hot. Makes 4 servings. Carb count varies according to choices made, roughly 10 carbs per serving.

Creamy Lemon Chicken*

*This recipe is not suitable for candida sufferers

This is one of those great recipes I learned from a retreat center I worked for during and after college. My husband and I actually went on staff there just four days after we were married! The place was just wonderful! It has a lake, a barn full of fun animals, and so many activities for both adults and children. Whenever I made this recipe, it always reminded me of that wonderful time of our lives. It is super easy and produces wonderful results. It has been a family favorite for years!

1 - 3 pound chicken, cut up
Seasoning salt, to taste
1 teaspoon grated lemon peel (lemon zest)
1/4 pound fresh mushrooms, sliced
2 tablespoons butter
1 cup cream
1 cup sour cream
1/4 cup chicken broth

Place the chicken into a large (9" by 13") baking dish. Sprinkle with seasoning salt and the grated lemon peel. In a medium frying pan over medium heat, cook the sliced mushrooms in butter until beginning to become translucent, about 5 minutes. Cool slightly, about 3 minutes. In a mixing bowl, using a wire whisk, thoroughly combine the cream and sour cream. Add the chicken broth and cooled mushrooms, mixing thoroughly. Spread all of the sauce over the chicken, so that the chicken is completely covered. Bake 2 hours at 350° F (or 1 hour if you prefer breasts). To serve, place excess sauce in a small serving dish and use as a gravy over chicken and your choice of veggie. Serves 4.

Carb count: Entire recipe, 20.84. Fiber, 1.26. ECC, 19.58.
Per serving, 5.21. Fiber, .32. ECC, 4.89.

Elegant Chicken*

*This recipe not suitable for candida sufferers

This would definitely impress company!

1 cut up chicken
Seasoning salt
1/2 pound bacon
10 medium (1 1/2") mushrooms
2 tablespoons butter
1/8 teaspoon basil
Garlic salt
1 cup grated Swiss cheese
1 cup half and half
Nutmeg

Place the chicken into a 9" by 13" baking pan. Sprinkle the chicken with seasoning salt to taste. Cut the bacon into 3" to 4" lengths. Place the slices over chicken, so that it is completely covered. Bake uncovered at 375° F for one hour.

Meanwhile, slice the mushrooms. Place the butter into a medium sauce pan and melt it over medium heat. Add the mushrooms and cook them until they are translucent, about 5 minutes. Add the basil and garlic salt to taste. Turn the heat to low and add the Swiss cheese and half and half to the mushroom mixture. Cook and stir over low heat until the cheese is thoroughly melted. Serve on individual plates, pouring sauce on each person's plate as they desire. Garnish with a tiny sprinkling of nutmeg. Serves 4.

Carb count: Entire recipe, 21.45. Fiber, 2.17. ECC, 19.28.
Per serving, 5.36. Fiber, .54. ECC, 4.82.

Fried Rice-aflower

This recipe is so far removed from the original Philippino recipe I learned from my friend! I didn't know if it would be an acceptable substitute for the "normal" fried rice. My son arrived at the table first. When he saw and smelled it, he said, "Oh! I know what this is! I LOVE this stuff!!" I said, "Well, no. We haven't actually had THIS before, but we've had something similar." Then my daughter said, "Fried rice!" I said, "Fried Rice-aflower..." Then they started eating. They all said, "Yum! Fried Rice!!" My daughter had three large helpings. It was definitely a winner!

1/2 head cauliflower (4 cups, chopped)
1 carrot
1/2 small (10") zucchini
2 stalks celery
Cooking oil
2 eggs
1/2 tablespoon chopped chives
1 1/4 pound pork or chicken, cooked (directions also given if meat is raw)
1 teaspoon seasoning salt
1/2 teaspoon lemon pepper
1 1/2 teaspoons sesame oil
1/4 teaspoon hot chili oil or a tiny pinch of cayenne
1 teaspoon lemon juice

Have a large mixing bowl available to place prepared veggies. Using a food processor with chopping blade, finely chop cauliflower florets with pulsing action, so they are the consistency of rice. Place the chopped cauliflower into the bowl. Using a shredding disk, shred the carrot and zucchini. Using the slicing disk, slice celery. Place all in bowl. (Or follow the same steps by hand.)

If the meat is cooked, use the slicing disk and slice meat. (If it is raw, cut it up by hand into 1/2" pieces.) Place the meat in a separate bowl.

Break the eggs into a small dish and season with a small amount of seasoning salt, beat set aside.

Heat a large wok or other large skillet over high heat with about 2 tablespoons of cooking oil to begin. When it is hot, add eggs to the wok, cooking until solid. Place the cooked eggs back into the bowl they had been in previously, and set aside. (If using raw meat, add a small amount of oil and the meat to the wok and cook it until it is no longer pink.) Add another 2 tablespoons of cooking oil to the wok and the prepared vegetables. Cook, using a scooping and lifting motion, bringing the cooked veggies up from the bottom so they become thoroughly mixed during the process. Cover and allow it to steam for a total of about 5 minutes, stirring about every 1 1/2 minutes. Add additional oil as necessary, so the vegetables don't scorch. When they are steaming and smelling good, add the egg, breaking it up as it is being added in. Stir. Add the meat and stir well. Season with seasoning salt, lemon pepper, sesame oil, hot chili oil and lemon juice. Taste and adjust seasonings if necessary (some like it hot, some like it saltier!) Serves 4.

Carb count: Entire recipe, 31.41. Fiber, 13.88. ECC, 17.53.
Per serving, 7.86. Fiber, 3.47. ECC, 4.39.

So what is all this business about "Carb count, Fiber and ECC?" If you've been low carbing for even more than a few minutes, you will understand the need to count our carbs. But what about the "Fiber and ECC" figures? Where do they fit into the picture? Some low carb plans allow their participants to deduct the dietary fiber from the total carbs of their food. The reasoning behind it is that since our bodies don't digest fiber, it shouldn't count into the carb count. They call this the "Effective Carb Count" or ECC. I am simply providing the information so that you can make well informed choices!

"Ham" Salad

I created this because with candida, I can't have ham. It always has sugar in it. Now, I can fool my mouth into believing that it is still getting one of it's favorite foods! I never know what is going to strike my 3 year old's fancy. Sometimes she surprises me. When I fixed this, she must have eaten 3 celery sticks stuffed full of "ham!"

1 pound Barbecue Pork (see recipe, p. 67)
2/3 cup Blender Mayonnaise (see recipe, p. 147)
1/2 tablespoon parsley
1 tablespoon onion flakes
1/4 teaspoon basil
1/2 teaspoon garlic salt
1/4 teaspoon dry mustard powder
1/4 teaspoon lemon pepper
1/4 teaspoon SteviaPlus® or 1/2 packet sucralose

Remove any visible fat from the Barbecue Pork. Place it into a food processor with a chopping blade, and process until the meat resembles fine crumbs. Place the chopped meat into a large mixing bowl. Add the remaining ingredients, and mix well. Serve with sliced cauliflower, celery sticks, zucchini or cucumber slices, or pork rinds for scooping. Serves 4.

Negligible carbs.

Hamburger Stew

Sometimes at the end of the pay period I look into my refrigerator and all I have left is some bits and pieces of this and that. It always seems that this is the time when I make this dish. It is hearty and satisfying. I don't feel quite so much like it is the end of a pay period then!

1 1/2 pounds ground beef
1 large Walla Walla Sweet onion, or any sweet onion, chopped
2 tablespoons cooking oil (canola preferred)
1 carrot, grated
2 cups cabbage, cut in 3/4" cubes
1 1/2 cups Beef Rich Stock (see recipe, p. 157) or commercially
        prepared, if no sugar (but not if you have candida)
Lemon Pepper
Garlic salt
1/2 tablespoon arrowroot mixed into 1/4 cup water

In a large skillet that has a cover, brown the ground beef over medium heat until it is no longer pink. Drain and set aside. Place the cooking oil into the skillet, add the onion and cook until the onion is translucent and is beginning to become golden brown around the edges, about 5 minutes. Stir in the grated carrot, cook for 1 minute. Add the cabbage, stock, lemon pepper and garlic salt to taste. Cover and simmer over medium-low heat for 30 minutes. When almost ready to serve, pour the arrowroot/water mixture into the stew, stirring until well combined. Serve in bowls. Makes 4 servings.

Carb count: Entire recipe, 34.29. Fiber, 7.22. ECC, 27.07.
Per serving, 8.57. Fiber, 1.8. ECC, 6.77.

Josephine's Spicy Spaghetti Sauce

My mother passed away over 10 years ago. When I found out I was going to be doing this book I knew I wanted to have this recipe in it! My sister said, "When I was a kid, this was a house-hold staple. Warn your guests or family that this is not Italian spaghetti, or they will be in for a shock! It was our favorite!!"

1 1/4 pound lean ground beef
1/2 medium onion (NOT the sweet variety)
1 stalk celery
2 cloves garlic
1/2 green bell pepper
1 cup Beef Stock (OR 1 teaspoon Worcestershire sauce, if you don't
      have candida)
2 - 8 ounce cans tomato sauce
1 - 15 ounce can diced tomatoes (no sugar!)
1/4 teaspoon salt
5 fennel seeds (anise seeds will work as well)
Heat:
      Either 1/8 teaspoon red pepper flakes, OR
      1 finely minced jalapeno pepper, OR
      several dashes tabasco sauce, OR
      3 dried chili peppers (1/2" long) OR
      all of the above if you like to eat fire!

Mince the garlic. Chop the onion, celery and pepper into 1/4" pieces. Crumble the beef into a large skillet and add prepared vegetables. Brown over medium heat, stirring frequently, until most of the red is gone from the meat, about 8 minutes. Add the Worcestershire sauce or concentrated beef stock, tomato sauce, salt and pepper, and "heat" of your choice. Simmer uncovered over medium-low heat until it is thickened, about 45 minutes. For a special meal, serve with Parmesan cheese over Slurp 'em Up Cabbage Noodles (see recipe, p. 138), or Baked Spaghetti Squash (see recipe, p. 115). Serves 4.

Carb count: Entire recipe, 59.64, Fiber, 12.97. ECC, 46.67.
Per serving, 14.91. Fiber, 3.24. ECC, 11.66.

Kentucky-Style Seasoning

Before I began the low carb way of life, I really enjoyed going to a particular fast-food chicken restaurant that has "secret spices." I did some research and found a recipe that I could use to make my own version of the regular fried chicken. Once I started low carbing, I knew I wanted to adapt it for this new way of eating. It does require a little effort in pulverizing the spices, but once that has been done, the seasoning mix will be good for months. I really think it is worth it!

Spice mixture:
1 tablespoon rosemary
1 tablespoon oregano
1 tablespoon sage
1 teaspoon ginger
1 teaspoon marjoram
1 1/2 teaspoon thyme
2 packets sucralose
1/4 teaspoon SteviaPlus®
3 tablespoons parsley
1/2 teaspoon lemon pepper
1/2 teaspoon pepper
1 tablespoon garlic salt
1/2 tablespoon garlic granules
3 tablespoons dehydrated onion
(1 tablespoon paprika, optional)

Coating ingredients: (Please see note on page 118)
Pork rinds
1 egg
2 tablespoons water
Cooking oil (canola preferred)

Place all of the ingredients for the spice mixture (first 15 ingredients) into a blender container. Blend on medium-high until it is completely pulverized into a fine powder. Store in an air-tight container.

To use:
Using a food processor, crush a hopper-full of pork rinds. Combine 1/2 tablespoon seasoning mix per each cup of crushed pork rinds used for breading.

Combine the egg and water in a shallow dish. Combine seasonings with the crushed pork rinds in another shallow dish. Coat the meat or veggies in the egg/water mixture and then in the rinds. Bake at 375° F or fry in cooking oil until done.

This is VERY versatile. It can be used as a deep fry coating for a variety of things: Chicken or pork nuggets, fried chicken, pork chops, beef or pork cubed steaks. It can also be used on various veggies, like eggplant, zucchini, onion rings, etc. It can, also, be used like the shaken and baked coating mixes without the egg/water. Place the desired amount of coating in a plastic bag and shake to coat pork chops, chicken pieces or chicken/pork nuggets. Then bake at 375° F until done: About 45 minutes for chicken, 25 minutes for pork chops or 10 to 15 minutes for nuggets.

This recipe yields MANY servings with negligible carbs.

Note: When using a cutting board or a knife, it is very important to avoid cross-contamination. For instance, if you are going to be cutting both meats and vegetables, cut the vegetables first and the meats last. Always wash and rinse your knives and cutting boards in the hottest soap and water available. You could save yourself and those you love from a nasty case of food poisoning by simply keeping your work area clean!

Lemony Beef and Asparagus Stir Fry

I served this to a dear gentleman who liked it so much he had thirds! He didn't say anything, but that was the biggest compliment he could have given my cooking! This recipe is VERY versatile. Substitute any meat for the beef and any appropriate veggies instead of the asparagus. Imagination and a great sauce are wonderful companions!

Sauce:
2 teaspoons arrowroot powder
1/2 large lemon, juiced (or about 1 1/2 tablespoon bottled lemon juice, but fresh is SO much better!)
3/4 cup Beef Rich Stock (see recipe p. 155) or commercially prepared with no sugar (but not if you have candida)
1/4 teaspoon ginger powder
1/4 teaspoon SteviaPlus® or 1/2 packet sucralose

1 1/2 pounds beef sirloin steak
1 1/2 pounds asparagus
4 large cloves garlic
(Optional: 3 carrots for non-low carbers)
Seasoning salt
Cooking oil (canola or peanut preferred)

Combine the ingredients for the sauce in a small bowl, and set aside. Heat a wok or large frying pan with about 1/4 cup of cooking oil over high heat. Quickly stir fry the garlic, then the meat. Add more oil if necessary and season the meat well with seasoning salt. Add the veggies to the wok and stir fry until crisp-tender, again adding oil if necessary, about 5 minutes. Add the sauce, turn off the heat and stir thoroughly. Serves 4.

Carb count: Entire recipe, 38.52. Fiber, 13.11. ECC, 25.4.
Per serving, 9.63. Fiber, 3.27. ECC, 6.35.

Marinated Lamb Barbecue

Why did it take 10 years after we left New Zealand for me to figure out how to cook lamb???

2 to 3 pounds lamb shoulder chops or ribs
1 teaspoon seasoning salt
2 tablespoons fresh mint leaves, finely chopped **
2 cups Beef Rich Stock (see recipe, p. 155) or commercially prepared, if no sugar, but if you have candida
Lemon pepper
Mesquite briquettes or chips, if using gas or electric barbecue

**Note: An unused mint tea bag may be opened and put into the marinade, if no fresh or dried mint is available. Just be sure it is plain mint, not infused with a lot of other ingredients that could effect the taste of the meat.

Place the meat into a large bowl with tightly fitting lid, and sprinkle with the seasoning salt. Add the mint and stock. Marinate for 4 hours to overnight.

Prepare barbecue. When the coals are to a white powder, or over medium heat, place the meat about 5" over the coals. Lightly season both sides of meat with lemon pepper. Cover and smoke the meat about 30 minutes.

I like to season the meat after it is over the coals so the excess seasonings fall onto the coals for some additional smoke flavor.

Enjoy this meat hot with a lot of napkins! Serves 4 to 6, depending on serving size.

No carbs.

Marvelous Meatballs

When my son sees that I am making meatballs, he runs through the house yelling, "We're having meatballs! We're having meatballs!!!"

1 pound Sharron's Pork Sausage (see recipe, p. 56) or
    1946 pork sausage (see recipe, p. 39)
1 1/2 pounds ground beef
3/4 cup ground pork rinds
1/4 cup onion, minced
2 tablespoons parsley
1/4 teaspoon dry mustard powder
1 teaspoon seasoning salt
3 cloves garlic, minced
1/4 teaspoon lemon pepper
2 eggs
1/3 cup Almond Milk, unsweetened (see recipe, p. 145) or cream (but
    not if you have candida)

Combine all of the ingredients in a large mixing bowl. Mix well and allow the meat mixture to rest at least 5 minutes. Form the meat into 2" balls. Bake them in a 9"x14"x2" baking pan about 20 minutes at 375° F, or barbecue over medium coals the same amount of time. They are done when they feel firm to the touch, no longer mushy. Makes about 26 meatballs. Serve with choice of dipping sauces. These can be placed in freezer bags and frozen for quick meals. Heat at 375° F about 25 minutes until hot.

I've tried doing this with my electric mixer, and the results just aren't satisfactory. There is just something about getting your hands in and kneading it by hand that the mixer can't duplicate. Just be prepared to get messy!

Carb count: Entire recipe, 18.62. Fiber, 6.71. ECC, 11.91.
Per meatball, .72. Fiber, .26. ECC, .46.

Mexican Beef Stew

I learned the Authentic Mexican version of this from some Hispanic friends during college. The mother of the family was an amazing cook, and I would often come in from helping at their farm to find a pot of this simmering on the back burner. It was wonderful!

1 1/2 pounds beef stew meat
2 tablespoons cooking oil (canola preferred)
2 large cloves garlic (1/2"x1")
1 medium onion
2 stalks celery
1 medium sized turnip
1 medium carrot (optional)
1/2 of a 8 ounce can tomato sauce (do NOT use the whole thing!)
1/2 teaspoon seasoning salt
1/8 teaspoon lemon pepper
1 teaspoon ground cumin
1/2 tomato
1 cup Beef Rich Stock (see recipe, p. 155) or commercially prepared
        with no sugar (but not if you have candida)
Low carb tortillas (optional)

Mince garlic, and chop other veggies into 3/4" cubes. Set aside. In a skillet that has a tightly fitting lid, brown the beef in oil over medium heat until the red is gone, about 3 minutes. Add the garlic and onions, continuing to cook and stir until the onions are translucent. Add the celery, turnip, (and carrot), cooking and stirring 2 minutes. Add the remaining ingredients, stirring to combine. Cover and simmer over low heat 1 hour. Remove the lid. Continue to simmer, and cook the sauce down until it is a thick gravy, about 20 minutes. Serve with low carb tortillas for scooping, if desired. Serves 4.

Carb count: Entire recipe, 32.49. Fiber, 7.95. ECC, 24.53.
Per serving, 8.12. Fiber, 1.98. ECC, 6.13.

Minted Lamb Chops

When my husband and I had been married for 5 years, we did an internship at a camp in New Zealand. It was a wonderful time, filled with fond memories! Recently, I found some adorable little lamb chops on sale. Oh, they were good! They reminded me of when my husband and I were in New Zealand.

1 pound lamb rib chops
3/4 cup Beef Rich Stock (see recipe, p. 155) or commercially prepared without sugar, but not if you have candida
2 tablespoons fresh mint leaves, chopped
Seasoning salt
Lemon pepper

Place the chops into 8" or 9" baking dish. Pour the stock over the top of the chops. Season liberally with seasoning salt and lemon pepper. Spread the chopped mint leaves over the top of the meat. Bake at 400° F for 25 minutes, until the juices run clear or a thermometer tests at 170° F. Serves 2 with no carbs.

I had trouble getting my thermometer to test properly because the chops were so tiny! It is really important not to let the thermometer touch the baking dish. That can give a false reading. If the thermometer is poked into the side of the meat, horizontally, then an accurate reading is possible.

Parsley Pork Steaks Macadamia

Sometimes I want a change of pace from the "same old" whatever! I had some pork steaks and didn't know what to do with them. This was the result. Pretty yummy!

2 pork steaks
1/3 cup ground macadamia nuts
1/3 cup crushed pork rinds
1/4 teaspoon lemon pepper
1 teaspoon chives
1 tablespoon parsley
1/2 teaspoon seasoning salt
1 egg
1 tablespoon water
2 tablespoons cooking oil (canola preferred)

In a food processor, crush the pork rinds. In a small shallow dish, place the ground macadamias, pork rinds, lemon pepper, chives, parsley and seasoning salt. In another small shallow dish, combine the egg and water. Pour the cooking oil into a 9" by 13" baking dish.

Coat steaks first in the egg/water mixture, then in the macadamia mixture. Be sure they are well coated. Gently place the coated steaks in the prepared baking pan. Bake at 375° F for about 30 minutes, or until meat thermometer tests at 170° F. Serves 2.

This is excellent served with Creamed Spinach With Macadamia Garnish (see recipe, p. 123)!

Carb Count: Entire recipe, 7.49. Fiber, 4.25. ECC, 3.24.
Per serving, 3.75. Fiber, 2.13. ECC, 1.62.

Pork Chops Kennewick

This is one of my sister's favorite recipes. It is a very popular dish around her place!

4 large pork chops, 3/4" thick
1 tablespoon cooking oil
1 large green bell pepper
4 large or 6 small cloves garlic
3 bay leaves
1 - 15 ounce can tomato sauce (no sugar added!)
Salt and pepper to taste

Place the pork chops and cooking oil into a large skillet. Cook over medium heat until the chops are beginning to brown, about 8 minutes. Meanwhile, cut the bell pepper into 1" cubes and coarsely chop the garlic. Add the bell pepper, garlic, bay leaves, tomato sauce, salt and pepper to the pork chops in the skillet. Simmer over medium-low heat until thickened, about 45 minutes. Prior to serving, remove the bay leaves. Serves 4.

Carb count: Entire recipe, 29.2. Fiber, 5.81. ECC, 23.39.
Per serving, 7.3. Fiber, 1.45. ECC, 5.85.

Rainbow Egg Salad

Yum! A nice change from ordinary egg salad.

2 hard boiled eggs
3 tablespoons Blender Mayonnaise (see recipe, p. 147) or commercially prepared (but not if you have candida)
Lemon pepper
Seasoning salt
Pinch celery seed
2 1/2 teaspoon of mixed dried veggies (includes spinach, celery, tomatoes, red bell peppers)

Crush the eggs in a small bowl. Add the remaining ingredients. Serve with celery, zucchini slices, cucumber slices, etc. for scooping. Serves one.

Tip for Homemade Lunch Meat:

A lot of folks are highly sensitive to the chemicals used in processed lunch meats. One alternative is to make a homemade lunch meat. It cannot be sliced thinly as deli meat is, but is more like a meatloaf in texture.

Purchase a couple of pounds of fatty pork, like country style ribs or pork steaks. Place them into a pan, cover them with water and simmer covered about 3 hours on low heat. The meat should be falling off the bone. Cool it to room temperature then remove the bones and huge chunks of fat from the meat. You will want to keep some of the fat so it will stick together! Finely chop the meat and fat so that it is uniform in texture. Place it into a bowl and pour in about 1/2 cup of the broth per pound of meat. Season with dried onions, seasoning salt, lemon pepper and basil. Combine thoroughly and taste. Adjust the seasonings as necessary. Place the meat intp a bowl with a flat bottom. Be sure to flatten the top of the meat. Chill it at least an hour, until the meat is solid. Remove the meat from the container, slice and serve. Negligible carbs.

Roast Leg of Lamb

My dear neighbor fixes this at every holiday. She gave me her recipe, and I had to modify it quite a bit. We served this to company and every one had at least seconds. The eldest daughter had four helpings and the dad had thirds. It was a huge hit!

6 to 7 pound leg of lamb (bone in)
1 clove elephant garlic, or 2 large cloves of garlic, slivered
1/2 cup olive oil
2 cups Rich Beef Stock (see recipe, p. 155) or commercially
        prepared without sugar if you don't have candida
3/4 cup lemon juice, bottled
2 tablespoons fresh lime juice
1 large sweet onion, sliced
1 carrot, sliced into 1/4" pieces
3 tablespoons parsley
2 teaspoons dried oregano leaves
1/4 teaspoon ground cloves
1 packet sucralose
1/4 teaspoon SteviaPlus® (use 3/4 teaspoon if your onion is hot)
1 teaspoon salt/lite salt
1 teaspoon seasoning salt

Rinse the meat under running water then place into a large baking dish. With a sharp paring or utility knife score the meat in many places. Insert a sliver of garlic into each score. Do this all over the meat on both sides. In a small bowl combine the remaining ingredients. Pour them over the lamb. Pile the vegetables on top of the meat. Allow it to marinate at least 24 hours, turning occasionally. Bring the meat to room temperature prior to roasting. Roast the lamb, fat side up at 325° F for about 3 hours, basting occasionally, until a meat thermometer inserted in the fleshy part reads 145° F. Remove the lamb from the oven, and allow it to rest about 20 minutes. Serve the vegetables and broth as a side dish. Serves 10.

Carb count: Entire recipe, 37.65. Fiber, 7.98. ECC, 29.67.
Per serving, 3.77. Fiber, .8. ECC, 2.97.

Salmon Patties

My husband and I recently went for our first a weekend away in many years to celebrate our 15th wedding anniversary. Our first night out, we were at a fancy restaurant overlooking the Columbia River. The view was incredible and the table intimate and romantic. There was a guitarist serenading us. My husband ordered their salmon patties. When he tasted them, he got this disgusted look on his face and said, "You know, you've really spoiled me! I like your's so much better!" I felt badly that he didn't like his dinner, but he made me a happy wife!

1 (14 oz.) can salmon, skin and large bones removed (be sure and rinse the tops of the cans!)
1 egg
1/2 cup crushed pork rinds
1/2 teaspoon dry mustard powder
1 teaspoon parsley flakes
1/2 teaspoon dill weed
1 1/2 tablespoon dried onion flakes, or 1/4 cup fresh minced onion
1 1/2 teaspoon lemon juice
1/8 teaspoon lemon pepper
1/4 teaspoon garlic salt
Cooking oil (canola preferred)

In a mixing bowl, combine all of the ingredients except the cooking oil. Mix well. Shape the mixture into patties about 3" across. Pour enough cooking oil into a large frying pan to completely cover the bottom and heat on medium. Carefully place the patties into the hot oil and fry until golden brown on each side, about 8 minutes total. Serve with Tartar Sauce (see recipe, p. 163). Serves 2.

Carb count: Entire recipe, 9.27. Fiber, 1.2. ECC, 8.07. Per serving, 4.63. Fiber, .6. ECC, 4.03.

Scampi

Just about every time we pass the seafood counter at the store, my kids ask if we can get shrimp, so we can have Scampi. Because of that, we've become friendly with the seafood manager. She's watched the weight coming off me and now she wants to do low carb!

3/4 pound shrimp/prawns, raw
2 large cloves garlic, minced
1 teaspoon seasoning salt
1 tablespoon parsley
1 1/2 tablespoon butter
2 tablespoons lemon juice

Peel and de-vein the shrimp. Rinse and place them fairly close together in a single layer in a shallow baking pan that can withstand broiling temperatures.

Warning: Do not use a glass pan!

Sprinkle the minced garlic, seasoning salt and parsley over the top of the shrimp. Break the butter into tiny pieces and put it on top of the shrimp. Pour the lemon juice over all. Broil for approximately 5 minutes, or until the shrimp has gone from being grey with black veins to being white with pink veins. Serve hot. Serves 4 with negligible carbs.

Seven Hill's Chili

Sometimes you just "need" some good, homemade chili! For those times, this is the one!

1 pound ground pork
1 pound ground beef (coarse ground for chili, if possible)
2 tablespoons dried onions
1 tablespoon dried garlic granules/powder
3 bay leaves
salt and pepper to taste
3 or 4 tablespoons chili powder
1 teaspoon oregano
2 teaspoons cumin
1 large (14 to 16 ounce) can chopped tomatoes (without sugar)
1/2 red bell pepper, chopped finely
1 small can (8 ounces) tomato sauce
2 tablespoons fresh parsley, chopped (fresh is best!)

In a large skillet with a lid, cook the pork and beef over medium heat until it is no longer red. Drain. Return the meat to the pan and add the remaining ingredients except the parsley (unless using dried, then add it at this time). Mix well. Cover and simmer over medium-low heat for 30 minutes. Add the fresh parsley and simmer 5 minutes. Serve hot in bowls. Serves 6.

Carb count: Entire recipe, 61.77. Fiber, 18.25. ECC, 43.52.
Per serving, 10.29. Fiber, 3.04. ECC, 7.25.

Crock Pot Tip: All the soup and stew recipes in this book are crock pot adaptable. Simply follow the instructions in the recipe. Place the ingredients in the crock pot, less any thickener, (as would be indicated in the recipe), and cook on low for about 10 to 12 hours (high about 6 to 8 hours). If the recipe uses arrowroot and water as the thickener, simply make sure the soup or stew is bubbling, and add it right in. If a recipe calls for no thickener on a conventional stove, you may wish to add 1/2 to 1 teaspoon arrowroot mixed into 1/4 cup water.

Sole Almondine

One day, I made most of the fish I had purchased as Sole Almondine, but also made a few pieces of basic batter fried fish for my husband. When my 9 year-old daughter had tried both of them, she said, "Oh I like THIS one so much better!" She had three pieces!

1 pound Dover sole fillets
1 cup blanched almonds, or slivered almonds
1 teaspoon seasoning salt
1 tablespoon parsley
1 egg
2 tablespoons water
1/3 cup cooking oil (canola preferred)
2 tablespoons butter
lemon juice, for serving

If using whole almonds, chop almonds in a food processor until they are coarsely ground. Do NOT chop the almonds until finely ground. If using almond slices, do not chop. Place chopped/sliced almonds into a shallow dish with the seasoning salt and parsley. In another shallow dish combine the egg and water.

Place the cooking oil and butter into a large skillet. Heat over medium heat until th butter melts. Meanwhile dip the fish fillets into the egg/water mixture, coating thoroughly, and quickly dip in almond mixture. This should yield a light coating of almonds. Fry the prepared fish quickly — about 1 1/2 minutes on each side. Do not overcook the fish. The fish will fall apart as it is removed from the pan if it is overcooked. Serve hot with freshly squeezed lemon juice. Serves 2.

Carb count: Entire recipe, 32.82. Fiber, 15.59. ECC, 17.23.
Per serving, 16.4. Fiber, 7.8. ECC, 8.62.

Spaghetti Squash with Cream Gravy

Rather like something from an Italian restaurant!

2 cloves garlic
1/4 teaspoon rosemary
1 tablespoon bacon grease or canola oil
3/4 pound cooked meat (lamb, pork, chicken, beef steak), sliced 1/4"
    thick and cut into bite-sized pieces
1/4 teaspoon salt/lite salt
1/8 teaspoon lemon pepper
1/3 cup unflavored Almond Milk (see recipe p. 145) OR cream (but
    not if you have candida)
Pinch nutmeg
1 tablespoon butter
1 cup cooked spaghetti squash (see recipe, p. 115)
1/4 teaspoon garlic salt
1/8 teaspoon lemon pepper
1 tablespoon water

In a medium skillet over medium heat, cook the garlic and rosemary in the bacon grease until the garlic begins to become translucent, about 3 minutes. Put the meat, salt and lemon pepper into the skillet. Cook and stir over medium-low heat until the flavors are well combined, about 10 minutes.

Meanwhile, in a medium saucepan over medium-low heat, melt the butter. Add the spaghetti squash, garlic salt, lemon pepper and water. Heat and stir until warmed through.

A few minutes before serving, pour the almond milk (or cream) into the pan with the meat. Cook and stir until the mixture is bubbling and beginning to thicken, about 2 or 3 minutes. Sprinkle nutmeg over top. Serve on individual plates. Place spaghetti squash on the bottom with gravy over top. Serves 2.

Carb count: Entire recipe, 22.63. Fiber, 7.32. ECC, 14.31.
Per serving, 11.31. Fiber, 3.66. ECC, 7.15.

Steam Boat

We went to visit some family friends for Thanksgiving, and they served this wonderful meal! This traditional Chinese feast, also called Hot Pot, is great for holidays, birthdays and other festive occasions.

Broth:
1 gallon Rich Stock (see recipe, p. 155), or commercially prepared vegetable or chicken stock (but not if you have candida)

Meat choices:
Chicken, pork, beef, shrimp, scallops, tofu, baby squid, lamb, duck, ham (sugar-free!), sole

Veggie choices:
Celery, napa (Chinese) cabbage, cabbage, carrots, green onions, spinach, bamboo shoots, snow peas, water chestnuts, mushrooms (but not if you have candida), zucchini

Optional:
2 - 10 ounce packages mung bean noodles (also called bean thread or cellophane noodles)

Condiments:
Fiery Hot Mustard (see recipe, p. 150), sesame oil, hot chili oil, minced garlic, sesame seeds, grated ginger root, chopped scallions, chopped cilantro, (soy sauce, vinegar, fish sauce, salsa, tabasco sauce and sherry, but not if you have candida)

Equipment needed:
Soup bowls, soup spoons, chop sticks, at least 2 wire mesh strainers per participant (available at Asian markets), one or two electric frying pans, large plastic table cloth

Cut the meat and veggie choices into 1/2" pieces. (Do not chop spinach.) The meat and veggie choices may be prepared the day before and stored in individual zipper sealed plastic bags or other covered containers.

Just before serving time, place the meats and veggies into serving dishes. Allow approximately 1/2 pound meat and at least 2 cups chopped vegetables per person. (Optional: Open mung bean noodles and soak in 2" cold water to soften.) In a large stock pot, warm stock over medium heat until hot.

Cover table with plastic table cloth for easy clean up!

Place the electric frying pan onto the dining table and fill with warmed stock to 1/2" below the rim of the pan. Turn the pan on medium-low heat, so that the stock remains hot. Place the meat and vegetable choices and condiments in serving dishes on table.

For the meal, each person fills their wire baskets with meats and veggies, (a different basket for each item), and places them into the steaming stock. The filled baskets remain in the stock until cooked – 1 to 3 minutes depending upon the item in the basket.

If using pork, be especially careful to cook it completely.

The host places spinach, napa cabbage and noodles into the electric frying pan without baskets. Each person places their cooked items plus any loose veggies or noodles desired in their soup bowls, with some additional broth, and the condiments of their choice. Continue this way until everyone has just about eaten their fill, about 1 to 2 hours.

The host needs to keep the pan full of broth and with ample supplies of noodles, cabbage and spinach.

At this point, there should be a lot of loose, cooked food floating in the broth. Beat the eggs in a small dish and pour into the steaming broth, stirring only one way for a final course of Egg Drop Soup. Serves 10. Use any leftover meats, veggies and broth to make some yummy soup. Carb count varies according to choices made.

Sue's Italian Chicken

My sister was grown and away from home by the time I was born. Some of my earliest memories are of going to her place when I was just a tiny little girl. She is a fabulous cook! She taught me much of what I know, and whenever I have a recipe question; she's the one I call on! This recipe reminds me of the wonderful spaghetti sauce she used to make when I was a child.

2 tablespoon cooking oil (canola preferred)
1 chicken, cut up
1 - 14 to 16 ounce can diced tomatoes (be sure it has no sugar!)
1 - 8 ounce can tomato sauce (again, no sugar!)
3 tablespoons Italian seasoning herb blend
3 cloves garlic, chopped
1 medium sized onion, chopped into 1" cubes
1 large rib celery, chopped into 1" pieces
1 small can green chilies, cut into 1" cubes (Or if you like it hot, 1
        jalapeno pepper diced finely)
Salt and pepper to taste

Place the cooking oil into a chicken fryer or other large covered skillet. Place the chicken topside down into the pan, and cook it until the meat is lightly browned over medium heat, about 8 minutes. Turn the chicken pieces over and add the remaining ingredients. Cover, and bring the sauce to a boil. Turn the heat to medium-low and allow it to simmer about 45 minutes. Serve piping hot in bowls. Serves 4.

Carb count: Entire recipe, 46.94. Fiber, 11.74. ECC, 35.19.
Per serving, 11.73. Fiber, 2.93. ECC, 8.79.

Sue's Pizza Sans Bread*

*This recipe not suitable for candida sufferers

"Sans" is just a French word that means "without." Enjoy this tasty pizza without guilt!

Sauce ingredients:
1 - 8 ounce can tomato sauce
1 teaspoon Italian seasonings (the combination that was used contains basil, sweet marjoram, parsley, garlic and red pepper flakes)
1/4 cup finely chopped onion or 1 tablespoon dried onions
1 bay leaf
1/4 teaspoon seasoning salt
Tiny pinch SteviaPlus® or sucralose

Crust ingredients:
1 1/4 pounds extra lean ground beef
1 teaspoon Italian seasonings (see above)
2 teaspoons dried onion flakes
1/4 teaspoon seasoning salt

Topping suggestions:
Sliced black olives
Thinly sliced bell pepper
Thinly sliced sweet onion
Cooked, crumbled bacon (sugar-free, of course!)
Thinly sliced salami (again, sugar-free)
Thinly slice pepperoni
Mushrooms
1/2 pound mozzarella cheese
1/4 cup freshly grated Parmesan cheese

In a small sauce pan combine the tomato sauce, Italian seasonings, onion, bay leaf, seasoning salt and SteviaPlus®. Simmer 15 minutes. Remove the pan from the heat and allow the sauce to cool completely.

In a mixing bowl, combine the beef, Italian seasonings, onion flakes and seasoning salt. Mix well. Press the beef mixture onto a round baking sheet to make the crust.

Be careful to form a rim around the edges so the toppings don't slide off as they bake!

Pour the sauce on top of crust and spread it evenly to the edges. Top with desired toppings. Sprinkle the mozzarella and Parmesan cheeses evenly over the top. Bake at 375° F for 15 to 20 minutes or until the cheese is bubbly and the meat is browned. Allow the pizza to rest for 3 to 5 minutes before cutting it into 4 slices. Serves 3.

My friend who tested this recipe thought it was simply wonderful!

Carb count: Entire recipe with all toppings suggested, 36.14. Fiber, 6.38. ECC, 29.76.
Per serving, 12.04. Fiber, 2.12. ECC, 9.92.
Entire recipe crust, sauce and cheese only, 32.46. Fiber, 10.06. ECC, 26.96.
Per serving crust, sauce and cheese only, 10.82. Fiber, 3.35. ECC, 7.46.

Surprise Meatloaf

This was a really fun recipe to create! I wouldn't allow my kids into the kitchen the day I made it for the very first time. I made a big deal of the "surprise" aspect of the recipe. It built up a lot of suspense and made it even more fun to eat. This would be a really special recipe to use for a birthday party or other special "kid-friendly" occasion!

1 1/4 pounds ground pork
1 1/4 pounds ground beef
1/3 cup Almond Milk, unflavored (see recipe, p. 145) or cream (but
    not if you have candida)
3/4 cup ground pork rinds
2 eggs
1/2 teaspoon hot chili oil or a pinch of cayenne
1 1/2 teaspoons seasoning salt
1 teaspoon lemon pepper
1 teaspoon sage
3 tablespoons dried onion flakes
3 tablespoons dried parsley
1 teaspoon dry mustard powder
1/4 teaspoon SteviaPlus® or 1 packet sucralose
4 eggs
Salt and pepper
1/3 cup Creamy Roasted Garlic Salad Dressing (see recipe, p. 149)
1 tablespoon dried parsley

In a large mixing bowl with an electric mixer, combine the pork, beef, almond milk, pork rinds, 2 eggs, hot chili oil, seasoning salt, lemon pepper, sage, onion flakes, 3 tablespoons parsley, dry mustard, and SteviaPlus®. Mix on low speed until thoroughly combined. Place the combined mixture into a 2 quart baking dish. Using the back of a 1/2 cup measure, press four holes into the top of the meatloaf. Break an egg into each hole and season the eggs with salt and pepper. Bake the meatloaf at 350° F for approximately 1 1/2 hours. Remove it from oven and spread the salad dressing evenly on top, covering up the egg "surprises." Sprinkle the parsley over all. Continue baking another 15 to 20 minutes. Use a spoon to scoop any excess grease from the top of the meatloaf. Serve hot. Easily feeds six.

Note: This recipe may also be divided into two smaller meatloaves, omitting the egg "surprises", one frozen for later use.

Safety Tip:
Meatloaf must be checked with a meat thermometer and test to 170 F for safety. E-coli is not something to be messed with! My father has almost died twice from it. The doctor's told him that once e-coli gets into a person's system as an infection, it never really goes all the way away. A simple precaution, such as always checking cooked ground meat with a thermometer is worth the effort!

Carb count: Entire recipe, 29.59. Fiber, 2.61. ECC, 26.98.
Per serving, 4.93. Fiber, .44. ECC, 4.49.

Tastes Like More Pork Roast

A very dear friend of the family popped in for lunch a while back. I had some leftover pork roast. He thoroughly enjoyed his first sandwich and said, "This Tastes Like More Pork Roast!" Hence, the name!

4 pound pork shoulder blade roast, or other boneless pork roast
    (If frozen, roast does not need to be thawed)
Seasoning salt
Lemon pepper
1 large Walla Walla Sweet onion, or other sweet onion, slice into 1/4"
    slices
3/4 cup Beef Rich Stock (see recipe, p. 155) or commercially
    prepared without sugar (but not if you have candida)
1 tablespoon arrowroot powder mixed into 1/2 cup water

Season all sides of the roast liberally with seasoning salt and sprinkle lightly with lemon pepper. Place the roast fat-side down in a large crock pot, (preferably with a removable crock.) Spread the onion slices evenly over surface of roast. Pour the stock into the bottom of the crock pot. Cover and cook on low for 12 hours. Allow it to cool 1 hour at room temperature then place the entire crock pot and its contents into the refrigerator overnight. About 1 hour before serving time, remove the crock from the refrigerator, and remove the fat that has separated from the roast and broth. Remove any large "debris" from the broth, and place the gelled broth and onion pieces into a medium sauce pan. Bring the broth to a boil over medium heat. Meanwhile, slice the roast on a plastic cutting board. Add the meat to the boiling broth, reduce heat to simmering and pour in arrowroot/water mixture, stirring lightly. Heat through, about 3 to 5 minutes. Serves 4. If a boneless roast is used, the meat may also be thinly sliced for deli-style lunch meat. Less expensive and better for us -- What a deal!

Carb count: Entire recipe, 20.85. Fiber, 3.15. ECC, 10.70.
Per serving, 5.21. Fiber, .79. ECC, 4.42.

Teeny Food

Eat the olives off the ends of your fingers! Have fun — this is the ultimate kid food. For a real treat, serve this off a child's tea set!

Choices of protein:
3/4 cup "Ham" Salad (see recipe, p. 80)
Tuna salad: 1 can tuna, drained mixed with 2 tablespoons Creamy Roasted Garlic Salad Dressing (see recipe, p. 149)
6 slices (ounces) cheese (not pasturized processed, and not if you have candida), cut into 1 1/2" pieces
6 slices deli-style lunch meat (sugar-free!), cut into 1 1/2" pieces
3 hot dogs, sliced (sugar-free)
Rainbow Egg Salad (see recipe, p. 92)
Egg Salad (see tip, p. 146)
Sardines
Nut Butter (see instructions, p. 181)

Choices of veggies:
1/2 cup olives
1/4 pound baby carrots (for non-low carbers)
3 stalks celery, cut into sticks
1/2 small zucchini, sliced
1 cup cauliflower, sliced
1/2 cucumber, sliced
1 cup radishes, sliced
Cabbage wedges, cut 1 1/2" by 2"

Prepare the choices of protein. Prepare the choices of veggies. Arrange each persons choices on their plates. The celery, zucchini, cauliflower, cucumber, radishes and cabbage wedges may all be used instead of crackers for bases for the protein choices. Note: Pork rinds or Crackers (see recipe, p. 120) may also be used as bases. Fill one celery stick with Nut Butter for each person. Serves 3 kids and one Mommy.

Carb count: Varies according to choices made.

Veggie Beef Stew

This makes a really nice hot lunch for cold, rainy days!

1 1/2 pounds beef stew meat
1 tablespoon cooking oil (canola preferred)
1/2 teaspoon seasoning salt
2 carrots, thinly sliced (optional)
1 1/2 cups shredded zucchini
1 clove elephant garlic or 2 large cloves regular garlic, finely minced
1/4 head cauliflower, thinly sliced
4" cut end from 1 bunch celery or 2 large stalks celery, thinly sliced
1/2 onion, thinly sliced
1/2 teaspoon seasoning salt
1/4 teaspoon lemon pepper
1 teaspoon parsley (fresh if possible), chopped
1/8 teaspoon lemon thyme (or a pinch – way less than 1/8 teaspoon
        -- of dried thyme, if no lemon thyme available)

In a 4 quart pot with a tightly fitting lid, brown the beef over medium heat in the cooking oil and 1/2 teaspoon seasoning salt, until the meat is no longer red. Cover the pot with a well fitting lid and simmer on low heat for one hour. Add the remaining ingredients, mixing thoroughly. Cover tightly, and simmer about 45 minutes. Serve hot in bowls. Serves 4.

Note: Please notice there is no additional water or thickener added to this recipe. A tightly fitting lid is an absolute essential for this dish! If your pan doesn't have a well-fitted lid, then the stew is likely to boil dry. Also, avoid opening the lid, especially in the early part of the cooking, since you don't want to lose any of the precious steam.

Carb count: Entire recipe, 50.5. Fiber, 18.29. ECC, 32.21.
Per serving, 12.62. Fiber, 4.57. ECC, 8.05.

Walla Walla Sweet Steaks

A girl from Washington State has to have a Walla Walla Sweet recipe doesn't she???

2 beef cubed steaks
1 medium Walla Walla Sweet onion (or if they aren't available, some other variety would do, I suppose!), cut into 1/4" slices
3 tablespoons cooking oil (canola preferred)
Seasoning salt
1 teaspoon arrowroot powder
1/2 cup water

Pour the cooking oil into a medium sized skillet and heat on medium heat. Season the steaks with seasoning salt to taste and carefully place in hot oil. Brown the steaks quickly on each side. Remove the steaks from the pan and set aside.

Add the onion slices to the hot oil. Season them to taste with seasoning salt, and cook them until they are beginning to become translucent, about 4 minutes. Carefully place the steaks on top of the onion slices. Also, place some of the onion slices atop the steaks. Cover the pan and turn the heat to low. Simmer 30 to 45 minutes. At this point, the steaks and sauce can be put in a storage container and refrigerated until ready to use.

When ready to use, heat the steaks and sauce back to a simmer. In a small cup, combine the arrowroot and water. Pour it into the sauce, stirring slightly to thicken. Serves 2.

This could easily be made with 4 or 5 steaks and still have enough gravy!

Carb count entire recipe, 15.29. Fiber, 2.7. ECC, 12.59
Carb count per serving, 7.64 ECC, 6.29

Washingtonian's Chicken*

*This recipe not suitable for candida sufferers

My sister's husband was quite eccentric.   He was a locksmith by trade, and they lived in an apartment attached to the locksmith shop for several years. He loved hamburgers. In fact, at one point in their marriage, he told her, "Why don't we eat hamburgers more often?" She made him hamburgers every day for a year before he started asking for anything else! He would absolutely not eat chicken. The one exception was this dish. He would not only eat it, he asked for it! Yummy!!

2 tablespoons butter
1/2 cup finely chopped fresh mushrooms (about 5 mushrooms)
1/2 cup heavy cream
1/4 teaspoon salt
Dash cayenne (much less than 1/8 teaspoon!)
1 1/4 cup sharp cheddar cheese, grated
6 boned, skinned, fresh chicken breasts halves (the largest available!)
1 egg, slightly beaten
2 tablespoons water
1/2 cup almonds
1/2 cup soy protein (NOT soy flour!)
Salt and pepper to taste

Cook the mushrooms in the butter in a medium sized skillet over medium heat until they are becoming translucent, about 5 minutes. Stir in the cream, salt and cayenne. Cook and stir over medium-low until the mixture has thickened. (The cream should be reduced by one-half.) Turn the heat to low and add the grated cheese, stirring until melted. Pour the sauce into an 8" or 9" square dish. Chill in the refrigerator one hour, then cut into 6 equal pieces (3 pieces across by 2 down), shaped like french fries.

Place each chicken breast between two sheets of plastic wrap and pound out from the center with a wooden mallet to form cutlets not quite 1/4" thick. Peel off the wrap and sprinkle the meat with salt to taste. Place the cheese sticks on each breast at the closest edge.

Tuck in sides and roll as for jelly roll.

Press to seal the chicken well — so the cheese won't run out all over the pan when it is baked!

Place the egg and water into a shallow dish and combine thoroughly. Set aside. Place the almonds into a food processor bowl and chop coarsely. Add the soy protein to the food processor bowl and continue chopping until the mixture is pulverized. Pour the ground almond mixture into another shallow dish and season to taste with seasoning salt. Dip the rolled breast halves first in the egg/water mixture then roll them in the almond mixture. Place the chicken onto a large baking sheet, cover and chill it in the refrigerator one hour or longer. Bake at 325° F for 45 minutes. Just before baking, drizzle the chicken with the melted butter and bake at 325° F for 45 minutes. Serve hot. Serves 6.

Variation:
Washingtonian's Chicken with Spinach filling: Instead of the mushrooms use approximately 1 cup fresh, chopped spinach. Follow all directions as written.

Carb count: Entire recipe, 27.54. Fiber, 12.58. ECC, 14.96.
Per serving, 4.59. Fiber, 2.09. ECC, 2.50.

Wonderful Chicken Club Pizza*

*This recipe not suitable for candida sufferers

The name says it all!

1 1/4 pounds ground chicken or ground turkey
1/2 cup crushed pork rinds
1 egg
1 tablespoon Italian seasonings
1/2 teaspoon seasoning salt

Sauce:
1/3 cup Creamy Roasted Garlic Salad Dressing (see recipe, p. 149)
        OR Creamy Ranch Salad Dressing (see recipe, p. 148)

Toppings:
4 slices cooked, crumbled bacon (sugar-free!)
3 medium mushrooms, sliced
4 olives, sliced
1/4 pound Monterey Jack cheese, grated
2 tablespoons freshly grated Parmesan cheese

Garnish:
Garlic salt
dried basil or oregano

In a mixing bowl combine the chicken, pork rinds, egg, Italian seasonings and seasoning salt. Mix thoroughly. Spread the mixture thinly on a round baking sheet. Leave a rim around the edge so the toppings don't fall off!

Spread the salad dressing over the chicken and place the toppings in order listed atop the dressing. Garnish with a gentle sprinkling of garlic salt and a very light sprinkling of either basil or oregano. Bake at 375° F for 15 to 20 minutes, until the cheese is bubbling and the meat is beginning to brown. Allow to cool three minutes. Cut into four slices. Serves 2.

Carb count: Entire recipe, 6.87. Fiber, 1.64. ECC, 5.23.
Per serving, 3.44. Fiber, .82. ECC, 2.62.

Veggies, Sides and Snacks

Baked Winter Squash

When I was a child, my mother often made squash. I detested it! I called it "squish!" Now that I'm an adult AND have a decent recipe, I actually like it. Besides, squashes are great powerhouses for vitamins and minerals! They are a bit higher in carbs than normal low carb veggies, but no where near the total of yams or sweet potatoes. They can be used similarly, though. They make great bases for casseroles, gravies, and several recipes that are in this book. Enjoy an occasional treat of Baked Winter Squash!

1 medium sized squash (spaghetti, pumpkin or other "winter" variety squash)
Butter
Lemon pepper
Garlic salt or seasoning salt

Using a sharp utility knife, poke 8 to 10 holes total around then entire circumference of the squash. Place the squash on a baking sheet and bake it at 350° F for about an hour. Allow it to rest 5 to 10 minutes before cutting it in half lengthwise. Scoop out the seeds, rinse and allow them to air dry to use for Roasted Pumpkin Seeds (see recipe, p. 135). Scoop the squash flesh into a serving dish. Add a generous amount of butter, garlic salt and lemon pepper and mix well. (The amount of butter and seasonings will vary according to the size and type of squash cooked -- you will just have to taste it!) Servings vary according to size and type of squash.

Tip: To separate the "noodles" in spaghetti squash, use a large fork to scrape the flesh from the rind of the squash.

Variations:
Sweet Cinnamony Squash: Instead of lemon pepper and garlic salt, use approximately 1/2 teaspoon cinnamon, 1/4 teaspoon grated orange rind

(zest) and 1/8 teaspoon SteviaPlus® (or 1 packet sucralose) and 1/4 cup butter for a medium sized squash.

Baked Winter Squash Hash Browns: Cut the completely cooled squash flesh into 1/2" cubes. Heat enough cooking oil to cover the bottom of a 10" skillet. Add the desired amount of squash, (approximately 1 cup squash per person), to the oil. Season liberally with seasoning salt, lemon pepper, garlic granules and parsley flakes. Fry it over medium heat, turning every 5 minutes, until it is golden brown on all sides, about 20 minutes. Serve hot with butter or gravy of choice.

Way too yummy to be "diet food", but it is!

Any leftovers from firm-fleshed squash may be used for "I'm Eating It So Fast Because It Is So Good (a One Skillet Meal)," (see recipe, p. 47). Leftover spaghetti squash may be used in "Spaghetti Squash With Cream Gravy," (see recipe, p. 98).

Carb counts:
Spaghetti squash, 1 cup 10.01. Fiber, 2.17. ECC, 7.84.
Squash, winter, 1 cup 17.93. Fiber, 5.74. ECC, 12.19.

Breaded Zucchini

Breakfasts are sometimes difficult when low carbing. I usually eat eggs and some other breakfast meat, like sausage or bacon. There are times, though, when I just want something different! I feel so funny eating broccoli for breakfast, but I don't have any problems eating Breaded Zucchini or okra! My kids really enjoy it too! We also eat them for lunch and dinner.

1 small zucchini, or yellow summer squash, sliced about 1/8" thick
> Or 1 cup of any of the following may be substituted for the zucchini: Chopped frozen okra, sliced mushrooms (but not if you have candida), small broccoli flowers, onion rings, etc.

1 egg
1 tablespoon water
1 cup crushed pork rinds (see note*)
1/2 teaspoon garlic salt
1/2 tablespoon parsley flakes
1/4 teaspoon dried thyme flakes (optional)
Cooking oil (canola preferred)

In a small shallow dish, combine the egg and water. In another small shallow dish, combine the pork rinds, garlic salt, parsley (and thyme). In a large skillet, pour enough oil to cover the bottom to about 1/2." While oil is heating, dip zucchini slices in the egg/water mixture then into the pork rind mixture.

Hold the shallow dish with the pork rinds on its edge and shake gently while dropping the veggies in. This will provide an even coating without getting the GOO all over your fingers!

Gently place the coated pieces into the hot oil and cook on both sides until golden brown, about 3 minutes total. Serve hot with dipping sauces of choice. Serves 1 as a primary side dish or 2 as appetizers.

Individual Quick Freezing Tip: Place the cooked Breaded Zucchini pieces (or any of the other veggies suggested) on baking sheets sprayed with cooking oil spray. Place the filled baking sheet into the freezer until the veggies are frozen solid, usually over night. Store tightly sealed in freezer containers for up to a month. This makes a quick-to-heat veggie dish or appetizer. Just bake about 8 minutes at 375° F and enjoy!

Note of caution: Once, I decided to not pre-cook the Breaded Zucchini before freezing it. I had hoped to save myself from cooking them twice. I did a huge batch of yellow summer squash and zucchini. I froze them on the trays and put them in freezer in bags. Major disaster! When I cooked them, the breading fell off and the squash got slimy. Yuck! What a waste of perfectly good food.

Carb count: Entire recipe (zucchini), 4.7. Fiber, 1.55. ECC, 3.15.

*For those who are frugal: You may add 1 tablespoons of soy protein (NOT soy flour!), per cup of the pork rind breading mixture on both this recipe and Kentucky-Style Seasoning (see recipe, p. 83) in order to make the breading coat more pieces of food. The coating doesn't turn out as thick and crunchy, but it does make it last longer and coat more pieces. When finances are tight, it makes sense and cents to get as much out of the recipe as you can!

Clam Cakes

I am never quite sure what food is going to please my three year old. She really likes Clam Cakes! She always eats four or five of them! Besides making a great appetizer, they are good served alongside a salad for lunch.

1/2 pound chopped, fresh clams (or equivalent canned clams, without sugar, drained)
1 egg
1 tablespoon water
2/3 cup ground pork rinds
1/2 teaspoon lemon juice
1 tablespoon parsley flakes
1/2 teaspoon garlic salt
Dash lemon pepper (less than 1/8 teaspoon)
Cooking oil (canola preferred)
Lemon juice for serving

In a mixing bowl, combine the clams, egg, water, pork rinds, lemon juice, parsley, garlic salt and lemon pepper. Combine thoroughly and allow the mixture to rest for 3 to 5 minutes. Pour about 3 tablespoons of cooking oil into the bottom of a large skillet. Heat over medium heat until hot. Form the clam mixture into 1 1/2" patties and fry them on each side in hot oil until they are deep golden brown, about 7 minutes total. Serve hot with lemon juice drizzled on top. Serves 4.

Note: Salad sized shrimp or chopped crabmeat may be substituted for the clams.

Carb count: Entire recipe, 2.7. Fiber, .56. ECC, 2.14.
Per serving, .67. Fiber, .14. ECC, .53.

Crackers

I live in the Pacific Northwest, where we have beautiful lakes and trees. There is a particular park that my family really enjoys visiting. It has huge douglas fir trees that look as if they are going to touch their tips to the sky, a beautiful lake, hiking trails and a great playground for the kids! We have seen wild ospreys, great blue herons, ducks and even caught little lizards. It is a really great park! One day my family had planned to go there for a picnic, and the meat I had was some left-over Surprise Meatloaf (see recipe, p. 104). I made meatloaf sandwiches on whole grain bread for my family, but I wasn't sure how I was going to manage mine! Pretty messy picnic fare! I decided I could probably create crackers using the same principles I had applied in my other baking — muffins, waffles, etc. It worked out great! The crackers were tasty and kept my fingers clean. My kids really enjoy them, too!

3/4 cup ground almonds
1/4 cup soy protein (NOT soy flour!)
1/2 teaspoon salt
1/4 teaspoon SteviaPlus® or 1/2 packet sucralose
1 tablespoon butter
1/4 cup Almond Milk (see recipe, p. 145) or cream, (but not if you have candida)
Seasoning salt

Using a food processor with a chopping blade, or by hand, combine the ground almonds, soy protein, salt, SteviaPlus® and butter. Pulse until well mixed. With the motor still running, pour in the almond milk (or cream) and process until the mixture is thoroughly combined. Remove the dough from the bowl and wrap it a sheet of plastic wrap. Set it aside for 10 minutes.

Sprinkle some soy protein onto a piece of waxed paper or other clean surface and place the dough on top. Roll with a rolling pin until thin, about 1/8".

Be careful not to roll them so thin that they fall apart!

Cut the rolled dough into squares, triangles or whatever shapes suit your imagination, so they are about 2 1/2" across. Use a spatula to move the crackers to an ungreased baking sheet. Sprinkle the crackers with seasoning salt. Bake at 325° F for 10 to 20 minutes, (keep an eye on them!), or until they are lightly browned on top. Makes about 20 crackers.

For easy clean up, simply roll up the waxed paper and discard!

Variations:
Crispy Crackers: Use canola oil instead of butter and water instead of almond milk.

Cheese Crackers: Use 1/2 cup ground almonds and 1/4 cup grated Parmesan cheese. Omit salt. Other ingredients and instructions remain the same.

Cinnamony-Sweet Crackers: Omit the salt in the mixing process. Add 3/4 teaspoon SteviaPlus® or 2 packets sucralose. Mix as directed. Instead of sprinkling the crackers with seasoning salt at the end, use 1/2 teaspoon SteviaPlus® or 1 packet sucralose mixed with 1/2 teaspoon cinnamon. Bake as directed.

Carb counts (basic recipe): Entire recipe, 17.49. Fiber, 9.98. ECC, 7.51.
Per Cracker, .87. Fiber, .49. ECC, .37.

Cream of Broccoli Soup

This makes a very nice accompaniment to lunch!

4 tablespoons chopped onion
1 tablespoon butter
2 cups Chicken Rich Stock (see recipe, p. 155) or commercially prepared broth without sugar (if you don't have candida)
2 cups broccoli (cut into 2" pieces)
1/2 teaspoon thyme
1 small bay leaf
1/4 teaspoon salt
Pinch pepper (way less than 1/8 teaspoon)
1/8 teaspoon garlic powder
1/2 cup Almond Milk (see recipe, p. 145) or cream (but not if you have candida)
1 teaspoon arrowroot powder mixed into 1/4 cup water (or about 1/2 teaspoon guar gum)

In a small sauce pan, over medium-low heat, cook the onion in the butter until it is translucent. Pour in the chicken broth. Add the broccoli, thyme, bay leaf, salt, pepper and garlic. Bring it to a boil over medium heat, then cover and allow it to simmer for 10 minutes. Remove the bay leaf and pour 1/2 of the hot mixture into a blender container. Cover the blender and place a towel over the top of the container to prevent a heat-induced blow-out. (It can be very dangerous!) Blend on medium speed 30 to 60 seconds or until it is smooth. Pour the soup back into sauce pan. Add the cream and arrowroot/water mixture and bring to a boil. Remove from heat and serve hot. Serves 2 as appetizers.

Variation: Cheesy Cream of Broccoli Soup – Add 1 ounce cheddar cheese before thickening, but not if you have candida.

Carb count: Entire recipe with arrowroot, 9.46. Fiber, 2.78. ECC, 6.68. Entire recipe with guar gum, 8.36. Fiber, 4.03. ECC, 4.33.

Creamed Spinach With Macadamia Garnish

This is a very elegant side dish!

1 pound fresh spinach, washed and trimmed of stems
1/3 cup Walla Walla Sweet onion, diced
2 tablespoons butter
1/2 cup Almond Milk (see recipe, p. 145) or cream (but not if you
    have candida)
Lemon pepper and seasoning salt, to taste
Pinch nutmeg (way less than 1/8 teaspoon)

Garnish ingredients:
1 tablespoon butter
2 tablespoons ground pork rinds
2 tablespoons ground macadamia nuts
1 1/2 teaspoons parsley
Garlic salt, to taste

Place the spinach into about 1/2" of water in a 3 quart pot with a lid.
Bring it to a boil over medium-high heat and turn the heat down to
medium-low. Cook it until it is done, about 5 minutes. Meanwhile, in
a small sauce pan over medium-low heat, cook the onion in 2
tablespoons butter. When the onion is translucent and beginning to
brown slightly around the edges, about 2 to 3 minutes, add the
Almond Milk and stir until thickened. Remove from heat. Add the
nutmeg and season with lemon pepper and seasoning salt to taste.

In a small frying pan, place 1 tablespoon butter. Melt it over medium
heat. Add the remaining garnish ingredients and cook and stir until
golden brown, about 3 to 4 minutes. Place the garnish in small
serving dish. Drain the spinach thoroughly. Place it into a serving
bowl and season it with seasoning salt. Break the spinach up so that
it isn't in a big ball, and pour the sauce over the spinach. Mix gently.
Garnish as desired at the table. Serves 4.

Carb Count: Entire recipe, 24.64. Fiber, 10.25. ECC, 14.39.
Per serving, 6.16. Fiber, 2.56. ECC, 3.59.

Deviled Eggs

What says "picnic" or "pot-luck" more than Deviled Eggs? I don't have a special dish that keeps the eggs from sliding around like some folks do for transporting them, though. Instead, I place a paper towel into the bottom of my serving dish before putting the eggs into it. This keeps the eggs from sliding about and also absorbs the excess moisture, so they stay nice and fresh.

12 eggs
1/2 cup Blender Mayonnaise (see recipe, p. 147) or commercially prepared (but not if you have candida)
1/8 teaspoon dry mustard powder
2 teaspoons onion flakes
10 drops (about 1/8 teaspoon) hot chili oil or a tiny pinch of cayenne
1/2 teaspoon seasoning salt
About 1 tablespoon dried parsley for garnish

Tip: When hard boiling eggs, put a pinch of salt in the water to keep the eggs from cracking.

Place the eggs into a sauce pan. Add enough water to cover the eggs, and bring it to a full boil. Reduce the heat, and simmer for 10 minutes. Drain the water and re-fill the pot with cold water to cool the eggs. Remove the shells from the eggs and slice the eggs in half, length-wise. Put the yolks into a small mixing bowl, and set the egg whites aside. Add the mayonnaise, mustard, onion, hot chili oil and seasoning salt to the yolks. Mix on medium speed with an electric mixer, or mix by hand, until the yolk mixture is smooth and creamy, about 2 minutes. Place the egg white halves on a serving plate. Fill the holes with the yolk mixture either using a piping tube or a teaspoon. Sprinkle a tiny amount of parsley over all when completed for a pretty finish. Serves 12.

Carb count: Entire recipe, 10.4. Fiber, .36. ECC, 10.04.
Per serving, .86. Fiber, .03. ECC, .83.

Egg Drop Soup

I think Egg Drop Soup is one of my favorite parts about going to an Asian restaurant. Now I can make it at home! This is great served as an appetizer before Barbecue Pork.

4 cups chicken or turkey Rich Stock (see recipe, p. 155) or commercially prepared broth without sugar (but not if you have candida)
1/3 cup frozen peas
1/4 cup finely chopped water chestnut
1 teaspoon arrowroot powder mixed into 1/4 cup water
Salt to taste
1 large egg

Place the stock into a medium-sized sauce pan over medium heat, and heat it just to the boiling point. While the stock is coming to heat, beat the egg in a small dish and set aside. When the stock is hot, add the peas and water chestnuts. Simmer 2 minutes. Add the arrowroot/water mixture and stir until the stock becomes clear again. Season with salt as desired. In a small stream, pour the egg into the simmering stock.

Use a large circular motion when pouring the egg in. Do it slowly over the entire surface area of the pan, but only in one direction. Also, stir only in one direction. This will keep the "egg flowers" from becoming "egg shreds." It takes a little bit of finesse, but it is worth it!

Serve immediately. Serves 4.

Carb count: Entire recipe, 10.53. Fiber, 2.06. ECC, 8.44
Per serving, 2.63. Fiber, .51. ECC, 2.11.

Egg Rolls*

*This recipe is for both low carb and non-low carb egg rolls

When I was in high school, my dad did a lot of cooking just for fun. He would decide that he wanted to try this or that, and just make it! He was really quite an extraordinary cook. One of the things he decided to try was Egg Rolls. We learned together and it is now a family favorite! I have taught my niece, and now I pass it along to you. This recipe is very involved, but it is SO worth it if you love egg rolls as my family does!!

6 cups cabbage, shredded
2 large carrots, shredded (not usually a low carb veggie, but I prefer
    the way the Egg Rolls look with them)
1/2 zucchini, shredded (optional)
1 small onion, grated (optional)
4 cloves garlic, minced
1 large broccoli stem, peeled and shredded
Other optional veggies include: Bean sprouts, water chestnuts, peas,
    mushrooms, (but not if you have candida), etc.
1/2 pound cooked meat (chicken, turkey, pork, beef or shrimp), or
    3/4 pound raw
Seasoning salt
Lemon pepper
Sesame oil
Hot chili oil
(Soy Sauce, if desired, but not if you have candida)
Oil for frying (canola or peanut are best for this job)
(Commercially prepared egg roll wraps, for non-low carb egg rolls)
Mountain Barley Bread™, for low carb egg roll wraps
1 tablespoon cornstarch mixed into 2 tablespoons water
Cooking oil spray

Equipment needed:
Wok or other large skillet
Large spatula
Large strainer and large bowl (durable plastic, preferred)

1/4 cup measuring cup
Very small bowl and a small spoon
Large cutting board or baking sheet
Kitchen towel, slightly dampened
Dinner plate or another cutting board
Kitchen scissors and tongs
Paper towels

Pour a about 1/3 cup cooking oil into the wok. Heat the oil and add the cabbage, carrots, zucchini, onion, garlic, broccoli and meat. (If your meat is raw, cook it FIRST and season it with seasoning salt, then add the veggies.) Cook on high, stirring constantly until the veggies are tender. Season the mixture liberally with seasoning salt, lemon pepper and sesame oil. Add a few drops of hot chili oil.

I've learned the hard way that you HAVE to taste this to get the seasonings just right! If it isn't perfect in the pan, it won't be perfect in the egg rolls...

Place a large strainer over a large mixing bowl and carefully place the cooked mixture into the strainer and allow it to cool.

If I am really organized and together, I'll get this done early in the day, or even the day before I'm to make the egg rolls. Unfortunately, I am rarely that on-the-ball! At this step, I am often found sticking the whole thing into my deep chest freezer and stirring it every 15 minutes to hasten cooling... The mixture has to be completely cooled to fill the wraps. If it isn't, it will melt the wraps, and that is not a pretty sight!

To use the Mountain Bread™ wraps, trim them to 6 1/2" squares. Set aside the excess bits for later use in Mountain Bread™ Crisps (see recipe, p. 131). Thoroughly wet the Mountain Bread™ under slowly running water. Allow them to rest for a minute or so before filling. This allows the bread to soften and become pliable enough for rolling.

Place on the workspace in front of you: The cutting board, cooled filling, damp towel, small bowl and spoon, dinner plate, scissors and Mountain Bread™, (or egg roll wraps). Directly in front of you, place the dinner plate. Mix the cornstarch/water in the small bowl with the spoon. (If using commercial egg roll wraps: Open the package on one end and use a dampened towel to cover the package opening and the cutting board where the finished egg rolls will be placed. They need to stay soft and pliable!) Place a wrapper diagonally on the plate. Measure 1/4 cup filling and place it in a "log roll" crossways slightly below center. (Figure 1) Fold up the bottom 1/3 of the wrapper. (Figure 2) Using the back of the spoon, spread a small amount of the cornstarch/water mixture around the edges of the wrapper wherever it will be touching other parts of the wrapper. This is the glue. Fold over the sides, so that it looks like a little pouch. (Figure 3) Seal the new edges. Using gentle pressure roll up, like a burrito. (Figure 4) Make sure it is very well sealed.

Any openings in the wrap will allow cooking oil into the inside of the egg roll, as well as letting the filling out into the oil to burn. Smells bad! Doesn't taste very nice, either.

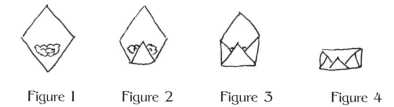

| Figure 1 | Figure 2 | Figure 3 | Figure 4 |

(Place each completed egg roll using commercially prepared wraps under the dampened towel on the cutting board.) For Mountain Bread™ wraps, place them uncovered on a baking sheet. When all egg rolls are completed to this point, they may be placed on baking sheets and individually frozen for later use. (See instructions for individually quick freezing, pp. 56 or 118).

(To cook the egg rolls using commercially prepared wrappers, fill the wok or frying pan with cooking oil about half full for deep frying. Heat the cooking oil to 375° F (hot oil) and cook the egg rolls until golden brown, about 3 minutes. Place on paper towels to drain.)

Arrange Mountain Bread™ egg rolls evenly on baking sheets. Carefully spray all of the surface areas of the Mountain Bread™ egg rolls with cooking oil spray. Bake at 375° F for about 15 minutes, until they are golden brown.

Serve the egg rolls hot with "Honey" Mustard Dipping Sauce (see recipe, p. 153), Fiery Hot Mustard (see recipe, p. 150), or Sweet and Sour Sauce, Low Carbed (see recipe, p. 162) and sesame seeds. Makes 24 total egg rolls.

Carb counts:
Filling: Entire recipe, 69.26. Fiber, 19.96. ECC, 49.3.
Filling per 1/24 recipe, 2.88. Fiber, .83. ECC, 2.05.
Mountain Bread™ wraps, per each entire slice, 9.52. Fiber, 3.8. ECC, 5.72.
Mountain Bread™ wraps, trimmed to 6 1/2" squares, 6.28. Fiber, 2.5. ECC, 3.78.
Total carb count per each Mountain Bread™ egg roll: 9.16. Fiber, 3.33. ECC, 5.83.

French-Style Green Beans

A wonderful way to serve fresh green beans!

1 1/2 pounds fresh green string beans
4 to 6 large cloves garlic, minced (about 2 tablespoons when
    chopped)
2 tablespoons butter
Seasoning salt

Wash the beans, and snap off the ends. On a cutting board with a very sharp utility knife, slice the beans into 3/4" to 1" pieces at a 45° angle. A lot of the interior of the bean should be exposed. Place the beans in about 1/2" of water in a 2 quart sauce pan with a tight fitting lid. Cover and cook them over medium-high heat for 8 minutes. Pour the beans into a colander. Run cold water over the beans in the colander to stop the beans from cooking any further.

In the same saucepan, melt the butter over medium-low heat. Add the garlic and cook it until it is just becoming golden. Do NOT overcook the garlic or it will become bitter! Add the beans back to the pan, season them to taste with seasoning salt and cook and stir until they are thoroughly heated. If a softer bean is preferred, the lid may be place on the pan and cooked for an additional 3 minutes. Serves 6.

Carb count: Entire recipe, 52.59. Fiber, 23.4. ECC, 29.17.
Per serving, 8.76. Fiber, 3.9. ECC, 4.86.

Note: The carb counts of green beans are higher than other low carb veggies. Be sure and allow for this during the day if you plan on having them for your evening meal.

Mountain Bread™ Crisps

These may be used as a stand alone appetizer or as a cracker or chip-base for spreading dips, egg salad, etc. Store leftover crisps in a bread bag tied loosely. They keep well for several days.

1 piece Mountain Bread™
Cooking oil (canola preferred)
Either: 1 teaspoon cinnamon mixed with 1/2 teaspoon SteviaPlus®
     or 2 packets sucralose
     OR Seasoning salt

Cut the Mountain Bread™ into 1 1/2" x 2" rectangles. Pour about 1/2" cooking oil into a large skillet. When the oil is hot, fry the Mountain Bread™ pieces on each side until golden brown, about 1 minute total. They will sizzle at first, then stop. When they stop sizzling, they are ready to be removed from the oil. Otherwise they become overdone very quickly. For a sweet treat, sprinkle the crisps with the cinnamon mixture. For savory crisps, season liberally with seasoning salt. Serves 2.

Carb count: Mountain Bread™ wraps, per each entire slice, 9.52. Fiber, 3.8. ECC, 5.72.
Per serving, 4.76. Fiber, 1.9. ECC, 2.86.

Tip for washing fruits and veggies:

I am sure you have seen the fancy "fruit and vegetable washes" around the stores like I have. They are rather expensive! If you are concerned about pesticides and other residue, there is a simple, safe alternative. Place 1 tablespoon distilled white vinegar into 1 gallon clean water. Simply immerse your fruits and vegetables in this wash and you will get the same results at a fraction of the cost!

Rice-aflower

I asked my 9 year old daughter, "What should I say about Rice-aflower?" She replied, "I like it much better than rice and potatoes. I don't like rice. I don't like potatoes!" This coming from a kid who just a couple of years ago lived on rice, potatoes and macaroni and cheese! Guess her tastes are changing for the better. Serve this as a base for your gravies and sauces.

1/2 head medium cauliflower
3 tablespoons butter
1/4 teaspoon seasoning salt
Dash lemon pepper (less than 1/8 teaspoon)

Cut the cauliflower in 2" chunks and place them into a small sauce pan with a tightly fitting lid. Pour about 1/2" water into the pan. Cover and bring it to a boil over medium heat. Turn the heat down and continue to boil slowly for 8 to 10 minutes or until the cauliflower pierces easily with a fork.

This will be cooked longer than the normal "crisp-tender" stage that would usually be done for cauliflower, BUT do not cook it until it is mushy!

When it is done cooking, drain the cauliflower in a colander. Place it into a small bowl with butter, seasoning salt and lemon pepper. Mash it with a potato masher until the cauliflower is the consistency and texture of rice. Serves 2.

Carb count: Entire recipe, 14.95. Fiber, 7.18. ECC, 7.76.
Per serving, 7.47. Fiber, 3.59. ECC, 3.88.

Roasted Pumpkin Seeds

Oooo! These are good! Save the seeds from Baked Winter Squash (see recipe, p. 115) after you've baked it. Rinse them, allow them to dry and then follow this recipe.

1 tablespoon cooking oil (canola preferred)
1/2 teaspoon fresh, snipped rosemary (or 1/4 teaspoon dried)
1/4 teaspoon fresh, snipped lemon thyme (or 1/8 teaspoon dried thyme leaves)
1/8 teaspoon lemon pepper
1/8 teaspoon garlic granules
3 drops hot chili oil or a tiny pinch of cayenne
1/3 cup raw, shelled pumpkin seeds (or any raw, shelled nut would work)
Seasoning salt, to taste

In a small frying pan, place the cooking oil, rosemary, lemon thyme, lemon pepper, garlic, and chili oil.

If you like your food hot and spicy, up to 1/2 teaspoon hot chili oil may be added at this time. Be aware the heat of this spice intensifies as it cools, so allow for this in your seasoning.

Warm the oil and spices over medium heat until the herbs begin to smell, about 1 1/2 minutes. Add the pumpkin seeds, stirring frequently until they loose their green hue and begin to turn very pale tan, about 1 1/2 minutes.

Do NOT over cook! If they become brown, all that will be left will be a hollow crispy "shell" of a seed!

Season with seasoning salt and enjoy! Serves 2.

Carb count: Entire recipe, 8.46. Fiber, 1.86. ECC, 6.6.
Per serving, 4.23. Fiber, .93. ECC, 3.3.

Roasted Veggies Over a Bonfire

These veggies turned out SO good! The onions were just wonderful! It always amazes me how everything tastes so much better when it is cooked outdoors.

1 large Walla Walla Sweet onion, or other sweet onion
2 small or 1 medium zucchini
1/4 teaspoon seasoning salt
1/8 teaspoon lemon pepper
2 tablespoons olive oil, or other cooking oil
Foil
Large bonfire, or other outdoors cooking fire

While your bonfire is getting to the red-hot coals stage, slice the veggies into 1/2" slices. Spread 2 large sheets of foil on a working surface, cross-wise on top of each other. Place the veggies into the center of the foil and season them with seasoning salt and lemon pepper. Drizzle the oil over all. Wrap the bundle tightly, squeezing out any excess air. Be sure there are no gaps in the foil. If there are any gaps, add another piece of foil to ensure there will be no leaks.

When the fire has reached the red-hot coal stage, gently place the veggie bundle into the coals for about 45 minutes, turning once part way through. Use a shovel or some other implement, to remove the veggie bundle from the fire. Allow the cooked vegetables to rest about 5 minutes. Carefully open the bundle, allowing the steam to escape. Serve hot with Bonfire Barbecue Steak (see recipe, p. 70). Serves 4.

Carb count: Entire recipe, 15.17. Fiber, 4.33. ECC, 10.84.
Per serving, 3.79. Fiber, 1.08. ECC, 2.71.

Rutabaga Chips

When I was looking up the nutrition information at the USDA database, I was amazed to find that rutabagas are excellent sources of calcium, potassium and vitamin A. I've also read they are very helpful in the healing process of candida infections. I thought that was some helpful information!

One medium sized rutabaga
Cooking oil (canola or sunflower preferred)
Seasoning salt

You have to have a food processor with a slicer for this one, since they are SO hard! I can't imagine trying to slice them by hand... Whack! Off goes a finger. Not a pretty thought!

Thinly slice the rutabaga into about 1 1/2" to 2" slices. Heat a 3 to 5 quart sauce pan half filled with water to a full, rolling boil. Carefully place the sliced rutabagas into the water and return to boiling. Boil the rutabaga slices for 5 minutes or until they begin to become slightly translucent. Pour them into a colander and pour cold running water over them. This stops the cooking process and allows them to cool completely.

In the same pot, with the water removed and the pot dried, or in a large deep fryer or wok, pour about 3" cooking oil. Heat the oil until it is very hot (375° F) and cook the slices about 6 minutes, turning occasionally until they are slightly dark. These chips get cooked slightly past what is "perfect color" for potato chips. They need the extra color because they start out darker. Drain them on paper towels and season with seasoning salt. They crisp up as they cool. Serves two adults, or one adult with three little kids!

Carb count: Total recipe, 31.38. Fiber, 9.65. ECC, 21.73
Per serving, 15.69. Fiber, 4.82. ECC, 10.87.

Sharron's Beef Jerky

What does one eat for snacks when one has candida? I had to come up with something! I talked with my sister at length about what sort of marinade we could use, since traditional beef jerky always uses soy sauce. After much discussion, we came up with this combination. My sister makes hers stronger by using more of all the seasonings. The recipe can be modified easily according to taste. I eat this for snacks almost every day. It is very sad when I run out of beef jerky!

3 1/2 to 4 pounds beef steak or roast**
4 tablespoons lime juice (fresh)
1/2 teaspoon garlic granules (or 1 clove garlic, minced)
1 1/2 teaspoon lemon pepper
1 tablespoon seasoning salt
1 tablespoon dried minced onion (or 1/4 cup fresh, minced)
1 teaspoon dried ginger
1/2 teaspoon dried mustard powder
1 teaspoon hot chili oil or a pinch of cayenne
1/8 to 1/4 teaspoon SteviaPlus® (or 1/2 to 2 packets sucralose)
        depending upon taste
1 1/2 cups Beef Rich Stock (see recipe, p. 155) or commercially
        prepared without sugar (but not if you have candida)

I've discovered that many different types of beef will work satisfactorily for beef jerky. The main thing is that it needs to NOT be heavily marbled. The marbling is fat which can go rancid after the drying process. Otherwise, any ol' cut of beef will work just fine. I've gotten super cheap roasts and they have done just as well as a London Broil!

Make thin slices of beef by slicing it at an angle across the grain of the meat.
Some prefer to partially freeze the meat before slicing, but I find that slicing at an angle with a very sharp knife does just fine. It may also be

possible to get the butcher to slice it for you for free when you buy it, but then you can't be so particular about getting the fat out. I save the trimmings in a zippered bag in the freezer for later use as Rich Stock (see recipe, p. 155).

Set the beef aside. Place the remaining ingredients into a large non-metal bowl with a lid, stirring well to combine. Add the beef, mixing thoroughly. Allow the meat to marinate refrigerated at least over night, turning and shaking the container occasionally to stir it.

If the meat is very fresh, it can be marinated up to 3 days. The flavors will intensify the longer it remains in the marinade.

When you are ready to dry the meat, lay it out on the drying racks of a food dehydrator. Discard the marinade. Dry the meat for about 4 to 6 hours. Alternatively, it may be dried on baking sheets in an oven set on the lowest setting for about 4 hours.

To test the jerky for doneness: The meat should no longer be mushy. It should be firm, but not crisp. Turn the dehydrator off when you believe it is getting close to being done and allow the meat to cool. It will continue to firm up as it cools. The jerky should be able to bend and show fibers when it is bent. That is how you will know when it is done. After this step, I usually have a few pieces that need a little more dehydration. I remove the pieces that are done drying and turn the machine back on for about 1/2 hour with the remaining pieces still in it. Then I turn it off and allow it to cool back down again. That usually finishes the job.

Store the jerky in a plastic bag in the refrigerator. Makes many snack-sized servings with negligible carbs.

Slurp 'Em Up Cabbage Noodles

Kid factor: They slurp just like noodles!

1/2 head cabbage
1/4 teaspoon lemon pepper
1/2 teaspoon seasoning salt
1/4 cup butter

Slice the cabbage into strips about 1/4" wide, so they resemble fettuccini noodles.

Individually separate the pieces of cabbage so that they are not in clumps or chunks. This will allow the water and steam to cook them evenly.

Place the sliced cabbage pieces into a sauce pan, (or steamer), with about 1/2" of water. Cover the pan with a tightly fitting lid, and cook the cabbage on medium heat for about 8 minutes or until it is tender.

They need to be slightly on the soft side — not the normal "crisp tender" you would want from a fresh vegetable — in order to achieve the "noodle" feel.

Drain the cabbage thoroughly. Place the butter into the bottom of a serving bowl and sprinkle the lemon pepper and seasoning salt over it. Add the cabbage, and mix it thoroughly with the butter and seasonings. Serves 6.

Carb count: Entire recipe, 24.65. Fiber, 10.44. ECC, 14.21.
Per serving, 4.1. Fiber, 1.74. ECC, 2.36.

Sweet Pumpkin Casserole

Think of that traditional Southern dish: Sweet Potato Casserole, and you've got the idea! It is so yummy — what a wonderful accompaniment to a great holiday meal.

1 - 29 ounce can pumpkin puree (about 3 cups)
1 teaspoon SteviaPlus ®
8 packets sucralose
1/4 teaspoon salt
2 eggs
1 1/2 teaspoons vanilla
1 cup Almond Milk (see recipe, p. 145), or cream (but not if you have candida)
Cooking oil spray

Topping:
1/2 teaspoon SteviaPlus ®
6 packets sucralose
1/2 cup soy protein (NOT soy flour!)
1/2 cup pecans (or any nuts)
3 tablespoons butter
1/2 teaspoon vanilla

In a large mixing bowl combine the pumpkin, sweeteners, salt, eggs, vanilla and almond milk. Mix thoroughly. Spay a casserole dish, pie pan or 8" square baking dish with cooking oil spray. Pour the pumpkin mixture into dish.

Place the topping ingredients into the bowl of a food processor and process until the mixture resembles coarse crumbs. (Alternatively, chop nuts by hand then combine all of the ingredients with a pastry blender until well combined.) Sprinkle the topping over the pumpkin mixture. Bake at 350° F until the topping begins to brown and the filling is beginning to set, about 35 to 45 minutes. Serves 8.

Carb count: Entire recipe, 83.28. Fiber, 29.64. ECC, 53.64.
Per serving, 10.41. Fiber, 3.7. ECC, 6.7.

Sweet and Spicy Almonds

The first time I made Sweet and Spicy Almonds, my kids smelled it from all the way across the street at the neighbors house. They all came running and begged for more after it was all gone!

1/2 tablespoon cooking oil (canola preferred)
1/4 teaspoon ground cinnamon
1/8 teaspoon SteviaPlus®
1 packet sucralose
1/3 cup blanched almonds
1/4 teaspoon grated orange rind (zest)
1/4 teaspoon almond extract

Place the cooking oil, cinnamon, SteviaPlus® and sucralose in small frying pan. Warm the oil and seasonings over medium heat about 1 minute. Add the almonds and heat them through, stirring frequently until the seasonings begin to really smell good and the almonds begin to get faintly darker than their normal white color, about 3 minutes. Remove the pan from the heat. Add the orange rind and almond extract, combining thoroughly. Pour the nuts into a serving dish and serve warm. Serves 2 unless the one has a real sweet tooth!

Carb count: Entire recipe, 10.39. Fiber, 5.02. ECC, 5.36.
Per serving, 5.19. Fiber, 2.51. ECC, 2.68.

Zucchi-Tater Pancakes

This really satisfies those "potato cravings" when they hit!

2 cups grated zucchini
2 tablespoons grated onion
2 small or 1 large clove garlic, grated
1 egg, slightly beaten
6 tablespoons soy protein (NOT soy flour)
1/2 tablespoon parsley flakes
1/2 teaspoon salt/lite salt
1/8 teaspoon lemon pepper
5 drops hot chili oil (about 1/8 teaspoon, but not quite) or a tiny
    pinch of cayenne
Bacon grease or canola oil
Butter (optional)
Seasoning salt (optional)

Using a food processor with a shredding/grating disk, (or by hand), grate the zucchini, onion and garlic. Place the egg into a mixing bowl, add the zucchini, onion and garlic and mix thoroughly. Add the soy protein, parsley, salt, lemon pepper and chili oil. Mix well and allow the mixture to rest about 5 minutes. Pour enough bacon grease into a large skillet to cover the bottom. Heat it over medium heat until it is hot. Using a 1/4 cup measuring cup, scoop the zucchini mixture into the hot pan. Fry the patties on each side until they are golden brown, about 8 minutes total. Add additional cooking oil as needed. Serve warm with butter and a sprinkling of seasoning salt (optional). Makes about 8 patties total. Serves 4.

Variations:
Spaghetti-Tater Pancakes: Use cooked spaghetti squash (or other Baked Winter Squash, see recipe, p. 115) instead of zucchini and reduce the soy protein to 3 tablespoons.

Cheesy-Tater Pancakes: Add 2 tablespoons grated Parmesan cheese, or 1/4 cup cottage cheese to the batter. Cook as directed.

Carb count: Entire recipe, 13.95. Fiber, 5.94. ECC, 8.01.
Per serving, 3.48. Fiber, 1.48. ECC, 2.

Zucchini Cakes

When I offered a taste of this to my darling husband, he refused. I told him, "They taste a lot like salmon patties..." He tasted and said, "Not too disgusting," and winked at me. I think that is pretty good coming from someone who is a die-hard zucchini hater!!

1/2 pound zucchini
1 egg
1 green onion
3/4 cup ground pork rinds
1/8 teaspoon lemon pepper
1/4 teaspoon garlic salt
1/8 teaspoon dill weed
1 tablespoon butter
1/4 cup cooking oil (canola preferred)

Using a food processor with grating disk, (or by hand), shred the zucchini. Using the chopping blade, (or by hand), mince the onion. Place the zucchini and onions into a mixing bowl and add the pork rinds, lemon pepper, garlic salt and dill weed.

Melt the butter and oil in a large skillet over medium heat. Shape the zucchini mixture into 1 1/2" patties and carefully place into the hot oil. Fry the patties until they are golden brown on each side, about 8 minutes total. Serve hot with sauces of choice. Serves 4.

Carb count: Entire recipe, 7.25. Fiber, 2.73. ECC, 4.51.
Per serving, 1.81. Fiber, .68. ECC, 1.12.

Salads, Dressings and Sauces

Almond Milk

"How in the world am I supposed to function on the candida restriction diet? How am I supposed to be able to cook without any dairy products at all?" Those were some of the questions that went through my mind when I first found out that I had candida. I looked at the various "milks" available in the health food section of the grocery store. All had some sort of sugar in them! So I went searching on the internet and found an almond milk recipe. I improved upon it and made it sugar-free. It has fewer carbs than cream and can be very useful to folks without candida for baking and sauces. For use in "savory" recipes rather than sweet, omit the flavorings. Just use the almonds and water.

1 cup raw almonds (or blanched, if available)
4 cups warm water
1/4 teaspoon SteviaPlus® or 1 packet sucralose
1 teaspoon vanilla
1/2 teaspoon almond extract

To blanch the almonds: Place the almonds into a microwave safe bowl, and pour in enough water to cover them. Microwave on high power for 2 to 3 minutes. The skins on the almonds should become loose and peel easily. Remove and discard the skins. Place the blanched almonds into a blender container and discard the blanching water. Pour the warm water into blender container, and begin to process the water and almonds on low speed, gradually turning the speed up to high.

When I start blending on high speed I end up with almond milk all over the kitchen!

Blend the almonds and water on high speed until completely smooth, about 3 to 4 minutes. Turn the blender off. Add the remaining ingredients through the hole in blender's top, blend (beginning on low again) until well combined. Place a clean towel, cheese cloth or paper towel into a strainer placed over a large bowl. Pour the Almond Milk into the cloth-lined strainer. Allow it to completely drain, pressing out as much excess liquid as possible. Pour the milk into a pitcher and store it in the refrigerator for up to 2 weeks. Save the "meal" leftover from the milk-making process and allow to air dry, stirring at least daily. If the climate is very warm or humid, this may need to be done in the oven or food dehydrator to prevent the meal from becoming rancid. This recipe yields about 1 quart almond milk and about 1/3 cup almond "meal".

Carb count: Approximately 3 carbs per cup almond milk. Almond "meal" has approximately 16 carbs per cup, about 12 fiber. ECC for meal, 4 carbs per cup.

Tip for yummy Egg Salad

Because I had candida, I needed to modify so many things in my diet! One thing that I had made that was very un-friendly to candida was egg salad. I made it the way my mother had: With commercial mayonnaise and sweet pickle relish. Commercial mayonnaise has vinegar, and sweet pickle relish has both vinegar and sugar! Vinegar and sugar are both "no-nos" with candida restriction. I had to discover an egg salad that was convenient and that everyone liked. I did, and know what? They like it better than the old way!

Simply combine 6 hard cooked eggs (see instructions, p. 126 for tips) with 1/3 cup Blender Mayonnaise (see recipe, p. 147), 1/2 tablespoon dried onion flakes, a sprinkling of each lemon pepper and seasoning salt, a teaspoon of parsley flakes and about 5 drops of hot chili oil. You may wish to adjust the seasonings to suit your own taste. This Egg Salad is very yummy stuffed in celery sticks or eaten on Crackers (see recipe, p. 120) About 5.74 carbs for the entire recipe.

Blender Mayonnaise

This does require some effort, but I've had even non-low carb friends tell me how much better this mayonnaise is than the commercially prepared type.

1 egg
1 teaspoon dry mustard
1 teaspoon salt/lite salt
3 or 4 drops hot chili oil OR a few grains of cayenne
1/4 teaspoon SteviaPlus® or 1 packet sucralose
1/4 cup olive oil
1/2 cup sunflower or peanut oil (safflower or canola acceptable)
3 tablespoons lemon juice (fresh is always best!)
1/2 cup canola oil (sunflower or safflower acceptable)

Coddle egg: Fill a small sauce pan with enough water to cover the egg. Bring the water to boiling, then gently place the egg into th boiling water for 20 seconds. Remove the egg from the boiling water, and immerse it in a bowl with ice-cold water to stop it from cooking any further.

Place the coddled egg, mustard, salt, hot chili oil and SteviaPlus® into a blender container. Blend on high until the mixture is well combined. With the blender still running, remove the center piece of the blender's lid and VERY SLOWLY, in a small stream, pour the olive oil into the egg mixture. Add the remaining ingredients in the order listed in the same manner. The mayonnaise will become very thick. The blender will need to be stopped periodically to stir the mayonnaise. Store it in a covered container in the refrigerator for up to two weeks. Yields many servings with negligible carbs.

Tips: If it is threatening to rain, don't try to make mayonnaise. It won't bind. You'll end up with a runny mess! Also, be sure you have a good, strong blender.

Adapted from "The Joy of Cooking."

Creamy Ranch Salad Dressing

Who would have ever thought I could have a creamy buttermilk ranch style salad dressing while being dairy free? I can now!

1 egg
2 teaspoons lemon juice
1 tablespoon dried onion flakes
1/2 tablespoon dried parsley flakes
1 teaspoon dried chives
1/8 teaspoon dried thyme flakes (not ground)
1/8 teaspoon celery seed
1/8 teaspoon dry mustard powder
1 teaspoon seasoning salt
1/8 teaspoon black pepper
3/4 cup olive oil (you may wish to use a mildly flavored one)
3 tablespoons water

Coddle egg: Fill a small sauce pan with enough water to cover the egg. Bring the water to boiling, then gently place the egg into the boiling water for 20 seconds. Remove the egg from the boiling water and immerse in ice-cold water to stop it from cooking any further.

Place the egg, lemon juice and seasonings into a blender container. Blend on medium speed until well combined. Stop the blender, and scrape the seasonings down from the sides of the container. With the blender running, pour the olive oil in a very small stream through the hole in the top of the blender container. Continue to blend and add the water. Turn blender to high and blend for about 1 minute more. Store in a tightly covered container in the refrigerator for up to two weeks. Yields about 1 cup, approximately 16 servings.

This makes a great dip, just use 1 1/2 tablespoons of water instead of 3 tablespoons.

Carb count: Entire recipe, 6.68. Fiber, 1.36. ECC, 5.32.
Per serving, .41. Fiber, .08. ECC, .33.

Creamy Roasted Garlic Salad Dressing

This has a very rich creamy texture and flavor, like a home made dressing at a very fancy restaurant!

1 egg
2 cloves Roasted Garlic (see recipe, p. 157)
1/8 teaspoon dry mustard powder
1 teaspoon seasoning salt
1/8 teaspoon black pepper
2 teaspoons lemon juice
3/4 cup olive oil (you may wish to use a mildly flavored one)
2 tablespoons water

Coddle egg: Fill a small sauce pan with enough water to cover the egg. Bring the water to boiling, then place the egg into the boiling water for 20 seconds. Remove the egg from the boiling water and immerse it in ice-cold water to stop it from cooking any further.

Place the Roasted Garlic into a blender container. Add the lemon juice, mustard powder, egg, seasoning salt and pepper. Blend on high until it is well combined. While the blender is still running, slowly pour the oil in a very thin stream into the hole in the top of the container. Add the water and continue to blend about 1 minute. Store refrigerated in a container with tightly fitting lid for up to two weeks. Yields about 1 cup, approximately 16 servings, with negligible carbs.

This also makes a great dip!

Variations:
Creamy Fresh Basil Salad Dressing: Substitute 6 - 1" fresh basil leaves and add 2 tablespoons fresh chopped chives instead of the Roasted Garlic.

Creamy Caesar Salad Dressing: Use 3 or 4 cloves Roasted Garlic and garnish your salad greens with freshly grated Parmesan cheese, but not if you have candida.

Fiery Hot Mustard

Although my father was an automobile mechanic for over 50 years, he could have been a brain surgeon or anything else he had wanted to be. He could fix anything and do anything. One thing he developed when he was nearing retirement was an avid love of cooking. He and I spent many evenings together preparing new foods. I still remember the time we tried to "bake" cookies in the microwave! Needless to say, that did NOT work. Most of his experiments did though, and this is one of them.

2 tablespoons ground mustard powder
1 1/2 tablespoons water

Simply combine the ingredients in a small bowl and enjoy in small amounts as a condiment. Serves 2.

Use this as a dipping sauce for Egg Rolls (see recipe, p. 126) and Barbecue Pork (see recipe, p. 67). Serve it alongside sesame seeds for a really "authentic" feeling Asian meal.

Carb count: Entire recipe, 6.9. Fiber, 2.88. ECC, 4.02.
Per serving, 3.45. Fiber, 1.44. ECC, 2.01.

French Salad Dressing

Sometimes low carbers need a change of pace from the basic ranch and caesar salad dressings they usually consume. This allows a very different choice!

1/2 cup tomato sauce
1/2 cup vinegar (or bottled lemon juice if you have candida)
1/4 cup lemon juice (fresh is best if available)
2 tablespoons minced dried onion (or 1/4 cup fresh)
2 teaspoons paprika
2 teaspoons seasoning salt
1 teaspoon SteviaPlus®
8 packets sucralose
1 cup cooking oil (olive preferred)

In a blender container, place the tomato sauce, vinegar, lemon juice, onion, paprika, seasoning salt, SteviaPlus® and sucralose. Combine thoroughly. With the motor running on medium speed, slowly drizzle the oil through the hole in the lid of the blender. Mix thoroughly. Makes about 16 servings.

This salad dressing also makes a wonderful marinade for chicken or pork!

Carb count: Entire recipe: 29.79. Fiber, 3.73. ECC, 26.06. Per serving, 1.86. Fiber, .23. ECC, 1.63

Variation:
Seafood Cocktail Sauce: Combine 1/2 cup French Salad Dressing with 3/4 teaspoon dill, 1 teaspoon horseradish (be sure that it is sugar-free!), 1/2 teaspoon garlic powder and 1/8 teaspoon black pepper. Serve with your favorite seafood.

Grown Ups' Guacamole

When I was in college, I was friends with several Hispanic families. It was at that time that I learned how to make this style of guacamole sauce. I just love it! It is called the Grown Ups Guacamole because my children prefer Kids' Guacamole (see recipe, p. 154). Usually any visiting adults prefer this one!

1 ripe avocado
1/2 small tomato, finely chopped, seeds removed
2 tablespoons fresh chopped sweet onion
1/4 teaspoon lemon juice
1/8 teaspoon garlic salt
1/8 teaspoon lemon pepper

Mash the avocado well in a small bowl.   Add the remaining ingredients, mixing well. Serve with salads, tacos, Mountain Bread Crisps (see recipe, p. 131), etc. Makes 2 large or 4 small servings.

Carb count: Entire recipe, 19.42. Fiber, 10.73. ECC, 8.69.
Per serving (2), 9.71. Fiber, 5.37. ECC, 4.34.

"Honey" Mustard Dipping Sauce

I've always wondered who created the first "whatever" — cake, pie, etc. Who discovered mayonnaise, for instance? From what I understand, most great recipes were discovered by accident. A fortunate combination of ingredients that were intended to be something entirely different, but turned out to be something entirely wonderful! This was one of those "I discovered it by accident" recipes. I was trying to make a candida friendly mustard/mayonnaise blend and ended up with this. I like it so much, I keep it on hand all the time!

1/4 cup Blender Mayonnaise (see recipe, p. 147) or commercially prepared mayonnaise (but not if you have candida)
2 1/2 teaspoons dry mustard powder
1/4 teaspoon SteviaPlus® or 1 packet sucralose
1/8 teaspoon garlic salt
1 1/2 teaspoons lemon juice (fresh is always best!)

In a small dish combine all of the ingredients mixing well. Store this sauce refrigerated in a covered container for up to two weeks. Serve with burgers, hot dogs, sausages, pork chops, Rutabaga Chips (see recipe, p. 135), Egg Rolls (see recipe, p. 126), Homemade Lunch Meat (see recipe, p. 92), etc. Serves 4 with negligible carbs.

Kids' Guacamole*

*This recipe is not suitable for candida sufferers

This is called Kids' Guacamole because this is the Guacamole for which my kids beg! Back before I began low carbing, I used to take my kids out to a local fast food taco place. Once I found out that I was allergic to just about everything there, that put an end to it. This recipe still allows them to have the guacamole they love so much.

1 ripe avocado
1/4 cup sour cream
1/4 teaspoon lemon juice
1/4 teaspoon seasoning salt

In a small bowl mash the avocado. Add the remaining ingredients and mix well. Serve with Mountain Bread Crisps, tacos, etc. Makes 4 small or 2 large servings.

This is great spread on Tostadas (see recipe, p. 208) for non-low carbers!

Carb count: Entire recipe, 17.31. Fiber, 10.05. ECC, 7.26. Per serving, 8.66. Fiber, 5.3. ECC, 3.36.

A good avocado, (if it is a dark skinned one), is just about black. It yields to gentle pressure, but is not mushy. It is rather like a peach in that respect. A good produce manager at a grocery or produce store should be able to help you find a nice one and learn how to check them. I've learned a lot from the produce manager at my local grocery store.

Rich Stock

This is one of my "basic kitchen necessity" recipes. I use it nearly every day, and it is a basic component for many of my soups and stews. It is also essential for Sharron's Beef Jerky (see recipe, p. 136), which I consider a mainstay of my diet! I usually make this after dinner with the bones, fat, skin left from the meal. I then allow it to cook all night on a back burner of my stove. I waken to yummy smells in the morning and my tummy is usually growling!

Approximately 3/4 pound beef or pork fat/trimmings and bones
      (the bones are really important!)
      OR 1 chicken or turkey carcass meat removed, leaving
      only skin and bones.
1 onion, peeled
2 carrots, peeled
2 large ribs celery
2 cloves garlic, peeled
2 bay leaves
Salt
2 tablespoons cooking oil (canola preferred), if doing Beef or
      Pork Rich Stock
5 to 9 quart stock pot with cover

For Beef or Pork Rich Stock: Place the cooking oil into the stock pot and brown fat, trimmings and bones over medium heat..

For Chicken/Turkey Rich Stock: Place the carcass into the stock pot.

For all: Cut the onion, carrots and celery in half. Place the onion, carrots, celery, garlic and bay leaves into the pot. Pour enough water to fill the pot with 3" of the rim. Cover the pot and bring it to a boil. Lower the heat until it is simmering very slowly, and allow it to cook for about 12 hours.

While this is simmering, a lot of foam and debris will come to the top. These are the impurities coming out of the stock. Remove them with a spoon and discard. The end result will be a wonderfully flavored, clear stock!

When the stock is a rich, golden color, it can be removed from the heat, salted to taste and allowed to cool. Alternatively, if a reduced, more intensely flavored stock is desired, remove the lid, increase the heat, and bring the stock back to a slow boil. Continue to boil the stock until it has cooked down 1/3 to 1/2 its original volume. How much you reduce the stock will depend upon how intense you want the flavor of the stock to. Add salt to taste.

Allow the stock to cool thoroughly, then strain it. Pour it into clean ice cube trays and freeze. After the stock has frozen, it can be then be placed into freezer containers or zippered freezer bags and stored for several months.

To use: Remove as much stock as is needed and thaw for use in recipes requiring broth.

Yields many servings with negligible carbs.

Roasted Garlic

Why roast a head of garlic? Raw garlic has an intense bite to it, and, when it is left raw in cold foods, the flavor grows more intense and overpowering as time passes. Roasted garlic on the other hand, has a rich, mellow flavor that doesn't compete with the food it is served alongside. It enhances it!

1 head garlic (yes, HEAD, not clove!)
1/2 tablespoon olive oil

With a sharp knife, cut the top 1/3 from the garlic, so that the insides of the cloves are all exposed. It may be necessary to individually cut some of the cloves if they are down farther in the head. Place the garlic into the center of an 8" square of aluminum foil. Drizzle the oil over the top. Wrap the foil around the garlic, then place it onto a baking sheet or other oven-safe dish and bake it at 325° F or 350° F for about 2 hours. This can be used as a spread for meat and vegetables or in recipes like Creamy Roasted Garlic Salad Dressing (see recipe, p. 149). It is also excellent spread on Barbecue Pork (see recipe, p. 67). Yields about 10 cloves of Roasted Garlic.

When I was discussing this recipe with my sister, she said, "There are as many ways to roast a head of garlic as there are heads of garlic!" She told me about one fellow who cooks his for 5 hours at 225° F. I can't afford the electricity! This method allows the garlic to be put into the oven with another dish, thus conserving energy.

Carb count: Entire recipe, 9.9. Fiber, .6. ECC, 9.3.
Per serving, .99. Fiber, .06. ECC, .93.

Scampi in an Avocado

My sister lives across the state from my family. She once came for a visit, when I had a ripe avocado and some cooked salad shrimp. I had a brainstorm, and this recipe resulted. We felt like we were eating at a very fancy restaurant! What a treat!

1 large avocado
2 small cloves or 1 large clove garlic, minced
2 tablespoons butter
1/2 tablespoon parsley flakes (one small sprig fresh parsley, chopped would be even better, if available!)
1/2 pound small salad shrimp (fresh, found in the deli-case)
1/2 teaspoon fresh lemon juice
Fresh parsley and lemon wedges for garnish, (optional)

Cut the avocado in half length-wise. Remove seed and gently remove skin. Place each avocado half on a plate.

In a medium skillet, melt the butter over medium-low heat. Add the garlic and cook it until the garlic is smelling wonderful and beginning to become translucent, about 2 minutes. Add the parsley flakes, cooking and stirring until heated through. Add the shrimp and lemon juice, continuing to cook until the mixture is heated through.

Do NOT over-cook the shrimp, or it will become rubbery. You just want it hot; it's already been cooked.

Pour the heated Scampi over the avocados, allowing the excess to spill onto the plates. Garnish with fresh parsley and lemon wedges if desired. Serves 2.

Carb count: Entire recipe, 17.5. Fiber, 10.91. ECC, 6.59.
Per serving, 8.75. Fiber, 5.46. ECC, 3.3.

Sesame Slaw

One day I had a head of cabbage, and I wanted some coleslaw. I didn't have the right ingredients to make my usual Yummy Coleslaw (see recipe, p. 164). I remembered a simple salad that my neighbor once served me that was based upon packaged ramen noodles and cabbage. The ramen noodles and their seasoning packet are not an option for me because of the candida restriction and the carb content of the noodles. I really enjoyed the flavor of her salad though, so I decided to be creative instead. This was the result!

2 cups shredded cabbage
1 tablespoon lemon juice (fresh is always best!)
2 tablespoons olive oil
1 teaspoon sesame oil
Pinch SteviaPlus® or sucralose (ever so much less than 1/8
    teaspoon!)
1 teaspoon fresh snipped chives (optional)
2 sprigs lemon thyme, chopped (optional)
1/2 teaspoon seasoning salt
1/4 teaspoon lemon pepper
1 tablespoon sesame seeds

Combine the lemon juice, olive oil, sesame oil, SteviaPlus®, chives and lemon thyme in a medium sized bowl, and mix well. Add the shredded cabbage and sesame seeds.   Toss well. Serves 4.

This would be great with Barbecued Pork (see recipe, p. 67)!

Carb counts: Total recipe, 7.6. Fiber, 3. ECC, 4.6.
Per serving, 1.9. Fiber, .75. ECC, 1.15.

Shrimp Salad in an Avocado

This wonderful salad is great for a special luncheon with a close friend!

1 large avocado
1/2 pound fresh salad shrimp (fresh, found in the deli-case)
2 1/2 tablespoons Blender Mayonnaise (see recipe, p. 147)
1/2 teaspoon fresh lemon juice
1 teaspoon dried onion flakes
1/2 teaspoon dried parsley flakes
1/4 teaspoon lemon pepper
1/4 teaspoon seasoning salt

Cut the avocado in half length-wise. Remove the seed and gently remove skin. Place each half onto a salad plate.

Combine all of the remaining ingredients in a small bowl. Mix well. Pile and equal portion of the shrimp salad on each avocado half, allowing the excess to spill onto the plates. Garnish each with fresh parsley or lemon wedges. Serves 2.

Carb count: Entire recipe, 16.77. Fiber, 10.05. ECC, 6.49.
Per serving, 8.38. Fiber, 5.14. ECC, 3.24.

Spinach Salad With Lemon Dressing

Can you say "five year old boy" and "spinach" in the same sentence? I sure can with this salad and my son! Whenever we have this salad he says, "Mommy, can I have more? I love this salad!" He makes me a happy mommy! This is such an easy, tasty dressing that I ask for lemon and oil whenever we go out to eat.

3 cups fresh spinach, washed and stemmed
8 black olives, sliced
1 tablespoon fresh lemon juice
1 1/2 tablespoons olive oil
1/4 teaspoon seasoning salt
1/8 teaspoon lemon pepper
2 tablespoons sunflower seeds

Optional additional ingredients:
1/2 tablespoon fresh chives
2 tablespoons fresh snipped parsley
1/4 cup freshly grated cheese (but not if you have candida)
3 slices cooked crumbled bacon (without sugar)
2 radishes, thinly sliced
1 green onion, sliced
1 hard boiled egg, sliced

Combine the spinach, chives, olives, lemon juice, olive oil, seasoning salt and lemon pepper in a serving bowl. Add any additional ingredients desired. Mix well. Garnish with hard boiled egg and sunflower seeds. Makes 4 servings.

Spinach Salad with Chicken or Pork: To make this salad into a single main dish serving add 1 cup chopped cooked chicken or pork to the above ingredients and use as many of the additional ingredients as possible. It makes a very satisfying lunch!

Carb count: Entire recipe, 10.11. Fiber, 6.07. ECC, 4.04.
Per serving, 2.53. Fiber, 1.52. ECC, 1.01.

Sweet and Sour Sauce, Low Carbed*

*This recipe is not suitable for candida sufferers

My husband and I were asked to create a program using a dinner and a movie theme. The movie the folks wanted us to use was about a lady who went to the Philippines. About 40 years ago, two young women went alone to live with a particular tribe. The chief "adopted" them for their protection. I learned this great recipe while I was studying to prepare myself to do those dinners.

1 tablespoon cider vinegar
1/4 teaspoon SteviaPlus®
1 packet sucralose
1/2 teaspoon salt/lite salt
1 tablespoon tomato sauce
3/4 cup water
1 tablespoon arrowroot powder mixed into 1/4 cup water

Combine the vinegar, SteviaPlus®, sucralose, salt, tomato sauce and water in a small sauce pan. Bring to boil over medium heat. Stir in arrowroot/water mixture and boil briefly until thickened.

Serve as a dipping sauce for Egg Rolls (see recipe, p. 126), Barbecue Pork (see recipe, p. 67), etc., or use as a basting sauce for chicken or pork. Yields about 6 servings.

Carb count: Entire recipe, 7.16. Fiber, n/a. ECC, 7.16.
Per serving, 1.19. Fiber, n/a. ECC, 1.19.

Tartar Sauce

Prior to discovering I had candida, I was a pickle fiend. I could easily eat a half jar of pickles in a sitting! I loved anything pickled: Cucumbers, beets, mixed vegetables, green beans, you name it! Now that I am on the candida restriction diet, I cannot have anything pickled or anything with vinegar in it. The tartar sauce I used to make was a basic combination of chopped pickles and mayonnaise. It took a little creativity to come up with a non-pickle version of Tartar Sauce that I could have with my restrictions and still enjoy. Now, my family likes this one better than the old way!

1/3 cup Blender Mayonnaise (see recipe, p. 147)
1 1/2 teaspoons minced dried onion
1 teaspoon lemon juice
1/4 teaspoon dried dill weed
1/8 teaspoon lemon pepper

Combine all of the ingredients and mix well. Store in a covered container in the refrigerator for up to two weeks.

Serve with Salmon Patties (see recipe, p. 94), fish, chicken or pork. Serves 4 with negligible carbs.

Yummy Coleslaw

I once brought this salad with all the options to a picnic. A non-low carb friend went nuts over it! My husband, who rarely even notices food, raved over the shrimp variation, too. I served it alongside Barbecued Pork, and he said, "Wow! What a Yummy dinner!" He made me a happy wife!

1/2 head small cabbage
Optional additions to salad:
1 1/2 teaspoons each snipped fresh garden herbs like lemon thyme, parsley, chives
1/8 teaspoon dried dill weed
3 ounces cooked salad shrimp (fresh, found in the deli-case)

Dressing:
1/2 cup Blender Mayonnaise (see recipe, p. 147) or commercially prepared mayonnaise (but not if you have candida)
1/4 cup Almond Milk (see recipe, p. 145) or cream (but not if you have candida)
2 tablespoons lemon juice
1/2 teaspoon SteviaPlus®
1 packet sucralose
1/4 teaspoon celery seed
1/2 teaspoon seasoning salt
1/8 teaspoon lemon pepper

In a food processor with slicing blade, or by hand, shred the cabbage. Place the shredded cabbage into a large bowl, adding any of the optional ingredients you desire. Set it aside. In a separate container, combine all of ingredients for the dressing. Add half of the dressing to the salad fixings, and stir well. Serves 6, with enough dressing leftover for one more salad. Store the extra dressing in a covered container in the refrigerator for up to two weeks.

Carb count: Approximately 22.8 carbs total. Fiber, 9.6. ECC, 13.2. Per serving 3.8. Fiber, 1.6. ECC, 2.2.

Desserts

Aimee's Original French Silk Pie, Low Carbed*

*This recipe is not suitable for candida sufferers

This pie is just incredible! I once served it to dinner guests, and after their first bite and all the ensuing "ooos and aaaahs," I informed them that it was sugar-free. Their mouths gaped open and their eyes bugged out! They said, "Well, don't tell the kids, they will never know the difference!" The husband still talks about how wonderful this dessert is.

Crust:
1 cup ground almonds
1/2 cup soy protein (NOT soy flour!)
1 teaspoon SteviaPlus®
4 packets sucralose
1/2 teaspoon cinnamon
6 tablespoons butter, room temperature

Filling:
3 ounces (squares) unsweetened baking chocolate (buy the best quality you can afford)
3/4 cup butter, room temperature
1 teaspoon SteviaPlus®
8 packets sucralose
1 1/2 teaspoons vanilla
3 eggs

Topping:
1 cup whipping cream
1/4 teaspoon SteviaPlus® or 1 1/2 packets sucralose
1 bar low carb chocolate

Crust instructions: Combine the crust ingredients with a pastry blender or food processor and press into a 9" pie pan. Bake it for 5 minutes at 450° F. Cool the crust completely before adding the filling.

Filling instructions: Break the chocolate into small pieces, and warm it in a small saucepan over the lowest possible heat. Stir it constantly, until it is almost completely melted. Remove the pan from the heat and continue to stir the chocolate until it is thoroughly melted. Allow the chocolate to cool completely.

Since the eggs won't be cooked, coddle the eggs: Fill a small sauce pan about half-full with water. Bring the water to boiling, then place the eggs into the boiling water for 20 seconds. Remove the eggs from the boiling water, and immerse them in ice-cold water to stop them from cooking any further.

In a large mixing bowl with an electric mixer, cream the butter, SteviaPlus® and sucralose on medium speed for about 1 minute. Add the chocolate and vanilla, mixing until combined. Continue mixing, adding the eggs one at a time and beating for 5 minutes each. The total mixing time for the filling will be 15 minutes. Pour the filling into the pie shell. Chill the pie for at least 4 hours to set.

Topping instructions: Whip the cream in a small mixing bowl with an electric mixer on medium-high speed until soft peaks form. Add the SteviaPlus® to the cream and whip it until it is combined. Spread the topping onto the chilled pie. Sliver the low carb chocolate bar with a vegetable peeler. Garnish the pie with the chocolate curls. Enjoy! Serves 8.

The original recipe came from Aimee Nossum. Thank you Aimee for letting me use this a really wonderful pie in my book!

Variation:
French Silk Cups: Omit the crust and prepare the filling as instructed. Pour the filling into muffin tins and chill. You may either top the French Silk Cups with the whipped cream topping as directed or serve plain. Makes 8.

Carb counts: Pie entire recipe, 64.87. Fiber, 28.07. ECC, 36.36
Pie per serving, 8.1. Fiber, 3.5. ECC, 4.54.
Cups entire recipe (without topping), 30.68. Fiber, 13.08. ECC, 17.6.
Cups per serving (without topping), 3.83. Fiber, 1.63. ECC, 2.2.

Cast of Thousands on Many Continents Chocolate Cake*

*This recipe is not suitable for candida sufferers

Maybe that is a stretch, but it certainly has had involvement from many different people in many different areas of the world! It was requested by a Korean lady who lives in Italy for her husband's birthday. Another lady who lives in California suggested this recipe because it was her best friend's mother's favorite recipe. Yet another gal who had recently moved from Europe, was living in Mississippi, and traveled to Chicago while in the testing process, came up with the brownie variation. I live in the Pacific Northwest. What wonderful teamwork! Serve this with Chocolate Cream Cheese frosting (see recipe, p. 171) for a yummy birthday treat!

1/2 cup ground almonds
3 tablespoons soy flour
1 1/2 tablespoons soy protein (NOT soy flour!)
1/4 teaspoon cream of tartar
1/4 teaspoon baking soda
1/4 teaspoon salt
1/4 teaspoon baking powder
1 egg, separated
1 teaspoon SteviaPlus®
4 packets sucralose
1/3 cup butter, room temperature
1 teaspoon vanilla
2 tablespoons cocoa powder
1/3 cup whipping cream

Line the bottom of a 9" cake pan with parchment paper, or spray the pan with cooking oil spray. Set it aside. In a small bowl combine the ground almonds, soy flour, soy protein, cream of tartar, baking soda, salt and baking powder. Set this aside. In a mixing bowl with an electric mixer on medium speed, beat the egg white until stiff but not dry. Set it aside.

In another bowl, with an electric mixer on medium speed, cream the SteviaPlus®, sucralose and butter, until they are light and fluffy, about 2 minutes. Add the vanilla, egg yolk and cocoa powder, beating well after each addition. Gradually add the dry ingredients alternately with the whipping cream, mixing until the batter is smooth after each addition. By hand, fold in the egg white. Pour into the prepared pan. Bake the cake at 350° F for about 20 minutes or until a toothpick inserted in the center comes out clean. Allow it to rest for 5 minutes, then invert it onto a rack to cool. When completely cooled, frost with Chocolate Cream Cheese Frosting, (see recipe, p. 171). Serves 6.

Variation:

Chocolate Brownies: Instead of separating the egg and beating the whites, use two whole eggs (not separated) and follow all of the remaining instructions. Frost or not according to preference.

Carb count: Entire recipe, 28.73. Fiber, 11.23. ECC, 17.5.
Per serving, 4.78. Fiber, 1.87. ECC, 2.91.

Chocolate Cream Cheese Frosting*

*This recipe is not suitable for candida sufferers

Both this recipe and the Chocolate Cake recipe came about at the request of a friend. She wanted something special to serve for her husband's birthday while still being low carb. Another friend gave me this recipe along with the cake that she has been saving ever since high school for something special. Husbands are special. Happy birthday!

1 1/2 tablespoons butter, room temperature
6 tablespoons cream cheese
2 1/2 tablespoons cocoa powder
3/4 teaspoon SteviaPlus®
6 packets sucralose
2 1/2 tablespoons cream
3/4 teaspoon vanilla

In a mixing bowl with an electric mixer on medium speed, cream the butter and cream cheese until they are light and fluffy. Add the cocoa, SteviaPlus®, sucralose, cream and vanilla, mixing well after each addition. Spread on Cast of Thousands on Many Continents Chocolate Cake, (see recipe, p. 170), or Pleasing Almond Macadamia Dessert, (see recipe, p. 185). Serves 6.

Carb count: Entire recipe 12.99. Fiber, 4.47. ECC, 8.52.
Per serving, 2.16. Fiber, .74. ECC, 1.42.

Coconut Macaroons

I love Coconut Macaroons! One day while I was thumbing through my copy of "The Joy of Cooking," I had the idea to adapt the recipe and make it candida-friendly. I really felt inspired when I came up with the substitute for the canned sweetened condensed milk! These sure taste like the "real thing!" They fooled my mouth!

1 cup Almond Milk, unflavored (see recipe p. 145)
1 teaspoon SteviaPlus®
8 packets sucralose
1 teaspoon vanilla
1/2 teaspoon almond extract
1/16 teaspoon salt (that is 1/2 of an 1/8 teaspoon)
2 egg whites
1 1/2 cups unsweetened shredded coconut

Place the Almond Milk into a small sauce pan. Cook and stir it over medium low heat for approximately 40 minutes, until the mixture is very, very thick and reduced to 1/3 cup. Stir in the SteviaPlus®, sucralose, vanilla, almond extract and salt. Put the mixture into the refrigerator for approximately 15 minutes to cool it completely.

In a small mixing bowl with an electric mixer on high speed, whip the egg whites until stiff peaks form. Set aside.

In a medium sized mixing bowl, combine the cooled almond milk mixture and coconut, stirring well. Fold in the egg whites. Scoop by teaspoonfuls onto a parchment lined baking sheet, about 1 1/2" apart. Bake at 350° F for 8 to 10 minutes. Makes 20 cookies.

Carb count: Entire recipe, 29.54. Fiber, 14. ECC, 15.54.
Per cookie, 1.47. Fiber, .7. ECC, .77.

Creamy Delicious Cheesecake*

*This recipe is not suitable for candida sufferers

Some occasions just cry for a special dessert. If you are a cheesecake lover, this is the one!

Crust:
1 cup raw almonds, ground
1/2 cup soy protein (NOT soy flour!)
1 teaspoon SteviaPlus®
4 packets sucralose
1/2 teaspoon cinnamon
6 tablespoons butter, room temperature

Filling:
2 large eggs, room temperature
3/4 pound cream cheese (NOT spreadable cream cheese in the tubs!), room temperature
1/2 teaspoon SteviaPlus®
5 packets sucralose
1/2 teaspoon vanilla (NOT imitation vanilla flavoring!)
1/2 teaspoon salt

Topping:
1 1/2 cups full fat cultured sour cream
1/8 teaspoon SteviaPlus®
3 packets sucralose
1/2 teaspoon vanilla (NOT imitation vanilla flavoring!)
1/8 teaspoon salt

Combine the crust ingredients well with a pastry blender or food processor and press into a 9" or 10" pie pan. Refrigerate the crust while preparing the filling.

Preheat the oven to 375° F. In a large mixing bowl with an electric mixer, beat the eggs. Add the remaining filling ingredients.

Be careful not to over mix the filling! It should be well combined but not over beaten. An over beaten filling will create a cheesecake with a poor texture.

Mix the filling ingredients until well combined, then gently pour the filling into the chilled crust. Bake at 375° F about 20 minutes. The sides of the cheesecake should be puffed, but the center should still be slightly jiggly. Turn the oven off and open the door, leaving it slightly ajar. Allow the cheesecake to cool in the oven for about 20 minutes. Remove the cheesecake from the oven, and place it on a wire cooling rack until it cools to room temperature.

It is very important to allow the cheesecake to cool completely between steps. It is also very important to bring the ingredients to room temperature before beginning to make this wonderful dessert. The texture will be adversely affected if the steps aren't followed properly. I figure, if I am going to go to the trouble of doing this cheesecake, I might as well do it right!

When the cheesecake is cool, preheat the oven to 425° F. In a mixing bowl combine the topping ingredients, and mix well. Pour the topping evenly over the cheesecake. Bake it for 5 minutes. Place it on a wire cooling rack and cool it completely to room temperature. Chill it in the refrigerator 6 to 12 hours before serving. Allow it to stand at room temperature 20 to 30 minutes prior to serving. Store any leftovers covered in the refrigerator. Serves 8.

Carb count: Entire recipe, 57.29. Fiber, 14.99. ECC, 42.3.
Per serving, 7.16. Fiber, 1,87. ECC, 5.28.

STOP THE PRESSES!!!

Just as this manuscript was going to print, I learned about a new sweetener on the market. It is all natural and may be substituted equally for the sucralose packets with the same carb count. It is Sweet & Slender™ by Wisdom Herbs. For more information and to purchase, please go to www.wisdomherbs.com.

Extra Special Egg Nog*
*Not suitable for candida sufferers

A wonderful treat for cold winter days. I often serve this after dinner instead of a regular dessert when we have company.

6 large eggs
2 cups cream (heavy whipping type if available) thinned with 2
     cups water (4 cups total liquid)
1/2 teaspoon SteviaPlus®
8 packets sucralose
1/4 teaspoon salt
2 teaspoons vanilla

Garnishes:
Chocolate curls (low carb, of course!)
Ground nutmeg and/or cinnamon

Since the eggs won't be cooked, coddle the eggs: Fill a small sauce pan about half-full. Bring the water to boiling, then gently place the eggs into boiling water for 20 seconds. Remove the eggs from the boiling water and immerse them in ice-cold water to stop them from cooking any further. Separate the eggs. Beat the egg whites with an electric mixer on medium-high speed until stiff peaks form. Set the yolks aside.

In a non-aluminum saucepan heat all of the thinned cream over medium heat for about 5 minutes, until it is beginning to steam. Do NOT allow the cream to boil! Pour the cream into a large non-aluminum bowl. In another bowl, beat together the eggs yolks, SteviaPlus ®, sucralose, salt and vanilla. Slowly pour the egg yolk mixture into the cream, whisking constantly with a wire whisk while pouring. Fold in the egg whites, combining well. Serve immediately. Garnish as desired in individual cups. Makes 1 1/2 quarts or 12 - 1/2 cup servings.

Carb count: Entire recipe, 22. Fiber, n/a. ECC, 22.
Per serving, 1.83. Fiber, n/a. ECC, 1.83.

Fake Fudge*

*This recipe is not suitable for candida sufferers

Have you ever had one of those days when you just need something sweet? You really don't care what it is, but another meal without dessert is just not what you want? That was how this recipe came about. If you don't have candida, it is completely "legal!" Before I learned I had candida, I used to make this recipe quite often. My kids still beg for it! They especially like the almond butter variation. I can quadruple this recipe, and they will still be licking the bowl at the end. Hope you enjoy it, too!

2 tablespoons cream cheese
1/2 tablespoon cream
1 packet sucralose
1/4 teaspoon SteviaPlus®
1/2 tablespoon cocoa powder

Place the cream cheese into a small microwave safe dish and warm for about 20 seconds in the microwave. Add the cream, sucralose, SteviaPlus® and cocoa powder. Mix it well and eat it off of a spoon! Serves one.

Carb count: Entire recipe, 3.63. Fiber, .89. ECC, 2.79.

Variation:
Peanut Butter Fudge: This can be made by adding 1 tablespoon Nut Butter (see instructions, p. 181) of any variety — though almond is especially nice! — stirred in with or without the cocoa powder.

Holiday Caramels*

Every year at Christmastime when I was a child, my sister made caramels as gifts for all of her family and friends. One year, a huge shirtless man, covered in tattoos, wandered in her back door while she was making some of those trademark caramels. She politely asked him why he was in her house. He replied that he had smelled an amazing smell, and he just had to know from where it was coming. He'd followed his nose right in her back door! Even with his tough-guy appearance, he turned out to be a life-long friend. All because of caramels.

2 cups heavy whipping cream
1 teaspoon SteviaPlus ®
8 packets sucralose
2 teaspoons vanilla

Place all of the ingredients into a small saucepan. Cook and stir over medium heat until mixture becomes very thick and ultimately begins to break apart.

This process will take approximately one hour. You will need to be patient and keep cooking until the thick caramel mixture starts breaking up into clumps. If you don't the caramels will still be quite tasty, but they won't set up!

Pour the caramel mixture into an 8" square dish and refrigerate. When completely cooled, cut into 20 squares. 20 servings.

Carb count: Entire recipe, 14.34. Fiber, n/a. ECC, 14.34. Per serving, .71. Fiber, n/a. ECC, .71.

Lemon Chess Custard

I took this dessert to my birthday party and had it while everyone else was having cake and ice cream in my honor. I didn't feel deprived at all!

4 eggs
1/2 tablespoon SteviaPlus®
4 packets sucralose
3/4 cup almond milk (see recipe, p. 145) or 1/2 cup cream thinned
        to 3/4 cup (if you don't have candida)
1/4 cup melted butter
1 teaspoon grated lemon rind (zest)
2 tablespoons lemon juice (fresh is always best!)
1/2 tablespoon arrowroot powder
1 tablespoon ground almonds (optional)
1 1/2 teaspoons vanilla

In a mixing bowl beat eggs. Add remaining ingredients and mix well. Pour into a small (8" or 9") pie plate that has been sprayed with cooking spray. Place in an oven that has been preheated to 350° F. Bake about 25 minutes or until a knife inserted off center comes out clean. Place on a wire rack to cool. Serves 8.

Carb count: Entire recipe, 14.8. Fiber, .95. ECC, 13.85.
Per serving, 1.85. Fiber, .11. ECC, 1.73.

Tip: There are many different varieties of vanilla extract. They can cost a few pennies to many dollars. I get my vanilla from a home distributor of cooking supplies. I highly recommend spending a little extra for REAL vanilla extract, rather than imitation vanilla flavoring. I really believe it is a big part of why everyone enjoys my homemade desserts so much!

Luscious Lemon Bars

This was definitely one of the more difficult-to-develop recipes! It took 6 or 7 tries to get it right, but I think it was worth it. Besides, we got to eat all those yummy Lemon Bars while I was trying to get it "just perfect!"

Crust:
6 tablespoons butter (room temperature)
1/4 teaspoon SteviaPlus®
3 packets sucralose
1/4 teaspoon almond extract
1/2 teaspoon guar gum
2 tablespoons soy protein (NOT soy protein!)
1 tablespoon water
1 cup ground almonds
Cooking oil spray

Topping:
3 eggs
1 1/2 teaspoons SteviaPlus®
5 packets sucralose
3/4 teaspoon guar gum
1/2 teaspoon grated lemon zest (peel)
1/4 cup lemon juice
1/2 teaspoon baking powder

Preheat the oven to 350° F. In a small mixing bowl with an electric mixer, cream the butter, SteviaPlus® and sucralose on medium speed until the butter is light and fluffy, about 1 minute. Add the almond extract, guar gum, soy protein, water and ground almonds, continuing to mix until it is thoroughly combined.

Spray an 8" or 9" baking dish with cooking oil spray. Using your fingers, press the crust into the dish. Bake it at 350° F for 15 minutes, until it is golden brown on top. Allow the crust to rest for 5 minutes.

The resting of the crust is terribly important! Once I didn't and the crust exploded when I poured on the topping! I stirred it together and we had "granola bars." They were yummy, but definitely not what I had planned!

While the crust is resting, crack the eggs into a clean mixing bowl. Mix well. Add the remaining topping ingredients one at a time by sprinkling each gently over the top of the egg mixture and mixing on low speed after each addition.

It is really important to sprinkle the additions so that they are incorporated into the topping mixture individually. When I just dump it all in together, it makes little lumps. It is supposed to be smooth and creamy!

Gently pour the topping mixture over the crust and bake it at 350° F for 15 minutes. (Optional: When cooled you may sprinkle one packet sucralose over the top of the bars for a "sugar-sprinkled" appearance.) Cut into 9 pieces and serve warm from the oven or room temperature. 9 Servings.

Warm: They are very yummy, but the crust falls apart. Room temperature: Still yummy, but they don't fall apart! Your choice.

Carb count: Entire recipe, 37.39. Fiber, 15.36. ECC, 19.4.
Per serving, 4.15. Fiber, 1.7. ECC, 2.1.

A thought about "legal" sweets and treats while low carbing: It is really best not to have them daily. Over indulgence is what caused many of us to gain the excess weight in the first place! I suggest you save "legal" desserts and sweets for a once or twice a week treat.

Macadamia Nut Butter Cookies

The most fun part of this recipe is forming the balls of dough to make the cookies. My hands become quite gooey! Then, I get to lick them off. Yummmmmm...

1/4 cup macadamia nut butter (approximately 2 1/2 ounces macadamia nuts, whole)
1/4 cup butter, room temperature
1 teaspoon SteviaPlus®
4 packets sucralose
1/2 teaspoon vanilla
1 egg
1/2 teaspoon baking soda
1/4 cup soy protein (NOT soy flour!)
1/2 cup ground almonds

To make the nut butter: Place the nuts into food processor with chopping blade and process until they are creamy, about 2 to 4 minutes. At first, the nuts will form a meal, then the oil will begin to separate out of them. That is when the nut butter is formed.

In a small mixing bowl with an electric mixer on medium speed, cream the macadamia nut butter, butter, SteviaPlus® and sucralose for 2 minutes. Add the vanilla and egg, continuing to mix for 1 more minute. In a small bowl, mix the baking soda, soy protein and ground almonds. On low speed, gradually add the dry ingredients to the butter mixture, until thoroughly combined. The dough will be STICKY! Dust your fingers with soy protein and form the dough into balls about the size of golf balls. Place them 2" apart on a baking sheet, (lined with parchment paper, if desired, for easier clean-up), and bake at 375° F for 6 minutes. They should appear under-done. Allow the cookies to rest on the baking sheet for one to two minutes. Place cookies on a cooling rack to cool. Makes 9.

Carb count: Entire recipe, 38.19. Fiber, 12.83. ECC, 10.95.
Per serving, 4.24. Fiber, 1.42. ECC, 1.21.

Melt in Your Mouth Mousse*

*This recipe is not suitable for candida sufferers

This is one simple recipe that should be a part of every low carber's arsenal of "I'm dying for something sweet RIGHT NOW!" recipes. Quick to fix and extremely satisfying!

1 cup whipping cream
1 packet sucralose
1/4 teaspoon SteviaPlus®
Choose one flavoring

Flavoring:
1 tablespoon unsweetened cocoa powder plus 1/2 teaspoon vanilla or
        1/4 teaspoon cinnamon, or
1 teaspoon imitation maple flavoring, or
1 tablespoon lemon juice (fresh is always best!), or
1 1/2 teaspoons vanilla (optional, garnish with cinnamon)

Pour the cream into a mixing bowl and whip it with an electric mixer on high until soft peaks begin to form. Add the sucralose, SteviaPlus® and one of the flavorings. Mix until combined. 2 servings.

Be sure that the mixing bowl and beaters are at least room temperature. If they are hot from washing, or it is a hot day, put them into the refrigerator for a few minutes to chill. The cream will turn out lighter and fluffier that way! Also, be careful not to over-whip. You don't want sweetened butter!

Carb count: Entire recipe without flavoring, 6.64.
Per serving without flavoring, 3.32.
Cocoa mousse per serving, 4.78. Fiber, .89. ECC, 3.88.
Maple mousse per serving, 3.58.
Lemon mousse per serving, 4.65.
Vanilla mousse per serving, 4.08.

Meringue Kisses

Every year my husband's family has a reunion at a park that is owned by one of the family members. There is a big swing hung between two fir trees, a zip line and two rope swings. It is a great place for the kids to play with their cousins! This year I was aware of my son's allergies to sugar and wheat, plus I was low carbing. I made Meringue Kisses and took them to the reunion. They are very sweet and satisfying.

1/2 teaspoon SteviaPlus®
4 packets sucralose
2 teaspoons cinnamon
1/4 teaspoon nutmeg
3 egg whites
1/4 teaspoon cream of tartar
3/4 cup walnuts or pecans, broken into 1/2" pieces

Preheat the oven to 250° F. Place a piece of parchment paper onto a baking sheet, or spray it with cooking oil spray. Set aside. In a small bowl, combine the SteviaPlus®, sucralose, cinnamon and nutmeg. Set aside. In a medium-sized bowl with an electric mixer on medium-high speed, beat the egg whites with the cream of tartar until soft peaks form. Gradually beat in the cinnamon mixture until stiff peaks form. Fold in the nuts by hand. Drop by teaspoonfuls, about 1" apart onto prepared baking sheets. Bake for 35 to 40 minutes, or until dry.

Do NOT bake any longer than suggested. They will not look "done" because they are baked at such a low temperature.

Remove from baking sheets and cool completely on a wire rack. Store covered. Makes about 30 Kisses.

Carb count: Entire recipe, 18.75. Fiber, 7.27. ECC, 11.46.
Per serving, .62. Fiber, .24. ECC, .38.

Mmm Cookies

My three children and the neighbor boy all bit into these cookies at the same time. What I heard was a unanimous, "Mmm! These are good!!"

3/4 cup ground almonds
1/3 cup soy protein (NOT soy flour!)
1/4 teaspoon baking soda
1/4 teaspoon baking powder
1 teaspoon SteviaPlus®
6 packets sucralose
1/3 cup butter
1 egg
1 teaspoon vanilla
1/2 cup total additions
Additions:
Sugar free chocolate chips, broken walnut or pecan pieces, macadamia halves, hazelnuts, etc.

In a small bowl combine the ground almonds, soy protein, baking soda, baking powder, SteviaPlus® and sucralose. Set aside. In a small bowl with an electric mixer, cream the butter on medium speed for two minutes. Add the egg and vanilla, turning the speed to low and cream for one minute. Gradually add in dry ingredients by tablespoonfuls until combined. Stir in the additions by hand. Line a baking sheet with parchment paper. Form the dough into balls about the size of golf balls and place them approximately 2" apart onto the parchment. Tap the tops of cookies so that they will spread out, otherwise they will end up looking like little mountains! Bake at 375° F for 7 minutes. The should look slightly under done. Allow the cookies to rest on the baking sheet one minute, then put them on a cooling rack or paper towels to cool. Makes 9 cookies.

Carb count: Entire recipe, 21.11. Fiber, 10.37. ECC, 10.74.
Per serving, 2.34. Fiber, 1.15. ECC, 1.19.

Pleasing Almond Macadamia Dessert

When I made this I used raspberry flavored syrup, but many different variations of this could be made easily. Depending on what flavors of specialty syrup you have, your choices could range far and wide! My friend who tested this recipe for me has also ground the macadamias to butter and done it more like a brownie. Another variation she did was substituting soy flour for the macadamias. All have turned out yummy!

1 cup ground almonds
1/2 cup ground macadamia nuts
3/4 teaspoon SteviaPlus®
1/3 cup sugar-free flavored specialty syrup
3/4 cup Almond Milk (see recipe, p. 145) or 1/2 cup heavy cream
          thinned with water to make 3/4 cup (but not if you have
          candida)
1/3 cup butter (room temperature)
2 eggs
2 teaspoons baking powder
Cooking oil spray

Place all of the ingredients into a mixing bowl. On the lowest speed of a mixer, blend all ingredients until thoroughly combined. Turn the speed to medium, and beat the batter for 2 minutes, scraping the bowl often. It should become light and fluffy. Spray a 9" square cake pan with cooking oil spray. Pour the batter into the pan. Bake at 375° F for 20-25 minutes, or until the dessert tests clean with a tooth pick. Be careful not to open the oven too soon or it will fall! Place the dessert on a wire rack to cool. Serve it plain, sprinkled with a packet of sucralose, or spread with Chocolate Cream Cheese Frosting (see recipe, p. 171). Makes 9 servings.

Carb count: Entire recipe, 27.86. 13.66, fiber. ECC, 14.2.
Per serving, 3.09. 1.51, fiber. ECC, 1.57.

Pumpkin Cheesecake*

*This recipe not suitable for candida sufferers

Pumpkin is a great low carb veggie and makes a very special additions to this fine dessert. Great for the holidays!

Filling:
16 ounces cream cheese, softened
1/4 teaspoon SteviaPlus®
2 packets sucralose
3 eggs
1 (15 ounce) can solid packed pumpkin
1 teaspoon ginger
1/4 teaspoon nutmeg (or 1 1/4 teaspoon pumpkin pie spice, total if not using ginger/nutmeg)
Cooking oil spray

Topping:
2 cups sour cream
1/4 teaspoon SteviaPlus®
2 packets sucralose
1 teaspoon vanilla extract

Preheat the oven to 350° F. Coat the bottom of a 10 inch pie plate with pan spray. Set aside. In a mixing bowl with an electric mixer, cream the cream cheese, SteviaPlus® and sucralose. Add the eggs and mix lightly. Add the pumpkin, ginger and nutmeg, mixing well. Be careful not to over mix! Spoon the filling into the pie plate. Bake it for 50 minutes, or until a knife inserted off center comes out clean. Place the pan onto a cooling rack. Cool the cheesecake completely, then heat the to 400° F. For the topping, thoroughly combine the sour cream, SteviaPlus®, sucralose and vanilla and spread over the top of the cheesecake. Bake it for 8 minutes longer. Cool to room temperature on a wire rack. Chill, covered for 4 hours or over night. Allow it to stand at room temperature for 20 to 30 minutes before serving. Serves 8.

Carb count: Entire recipe, 70.35. Fiber, 12.65. ECC, 57.70.
Per serving, 8.79. Fiber, 1.58. ECC, 7.21.

Pumpkin Pie Pudding

We used this as a home school science project: One of the great things about desserts made with pumpkin is that it is actually a vegetable! It has a mild pumpkin pie flavor and is very yummy. My kid's gave the project an "A."

1 - 29 ounce can plain cooked pumpkin
3/4 teaspoon SteviaPlus®
6 packets sucralose
2 teaspoons pumpkin pie spice (or 1 teaspoon cinnamon, 1/2 teaspoon ginger, 1/2 teaspoon nutmeg)
1/2 teaspoon salt
3 eggs
1 cup Almond Milk (see recipe, p. 145) or 1 cup cream (but not if you have candida)
Cooking oil spray

In a mixing bowl combine the pumpkin, SteviaPlus®, sucralose, pumpkin pie spice and salt. Add the eggs and beat lightly. Add the Almond Milk, and mix well. Pour the pumpkin mixture into a 9" pie plate that has been sprayed with cooking oil spray, and bake it for 45 minutes at 375° F, or until a knife inserted off center comes out clean. Serve the pudding warm with almond milk or cream poured over the top. Makes 8 Servings.

Variation:
Pumpkin Pie Pudding with Coconut Milk: Substitute the Almond Milk with 1 - 14 ounce can coconut milk. Follow all of the remaining instructions.

Carb count: Entire recipe, 79.51. Fiber, 26.22. ECC, 53.29.
Per serving, 9.93. Fiber, 3.27. ECC, 6.66.

Silky Choco-Peanut Butter Pie*

*This recipe is not suitable for candida sufferers

Some things are just so yummy that it is hard to believe they are "diet" food!

Crust:
1 cup ground almonds
1/2 cup soy protein (NOT soy flour!)
1 teaspoon SteviaPlus®
4 packets sucralose
1/2 teaspoon cinnamon
6 tablespoons butter, room temperature

Filling:
1/2 cup sugar-free creamy peanut butter
3/4 cup butter, room temperature
1 teaspoon SteviaPlus®
8 packets sucralose
3 tablespoons cocoa powder
1 1/2 teaspoons vanilla
3 eggs

Topping:
1 cup whipping cream
1/4 teaspoon SteviaPlus® or 1 1/2 packets sucralose
Cinnamon

Crust instructions: Combine all of the ingredients well with a pastry blender or food processor and press the crust into a 9" pie pan. Bake it for 5 minutes at 450° F. Cool the crust completely before adding filling.

Filling instructions: Since the eggs won't be cooked, coddle the eggs -- Fill a small sauce pan about half-full with water. Bring it to a full boil, then gently place the eggs into the boiling water for 20 seconds. Remove the eggs from the boiling water, then immerse them in ice-cold water to stop them from cooking any further.

In a large mixing bowl with an electric mixer cream the peanut butter, butter, SteviaPlus® and sucralose on medium speed for about 1 minute. Add the cocoa powder and vanilla, mixing until combined. Continue mixing and beat in the eggs one at a time for 5 minutes each. Total mixing time for the filling will be 15 minutes. Pour the filling into the pie shell. Chill the pie for at least 4 hours to set.

Topping instructions: Whip the cream in a small mixing bowl with an electric mixer until soft peaks form. Add the SteviaPlus® and whip until it is combined. Spread the cream onto the chilled pie. Sprinkle the top of the pie with a dusting of cinnamon. Enjoy! Serves 8.

Variation:
Coconut Silk Pie: Omit the cocoa powder and peanut butter. At the end of the last 5 minutes of mixing, add 3/4 cup unsweetened shredded coconut, and mix until well combined. Follow the remaining instructions. Sprinkle with shredded coconut on top.

Carb count: Entire recipe (peanut butter) , 66.1. Fiber, 27.97. ECC, 38.13.
Per serving (peanut butter), 8.26. Fiber, 3.49. ECC, 4.77.

Ultimate Pumpkin Pie

My mother was never much of a cook. She always burned the pork chops, cooked the stew dry and put way too many peppers in her special spaghetti sauce (Josephine's Spicy Spaghetti Sauce, p. 84). In fact, many of the family recipes attributed to my mother were actually my father's ideas! One thing my mom did very well, though, was desserts. She baked incredibly light and fluffy cakes and wonderful pies with supremely flaky crusts. I loved the holidays. She always baked at least two different pies, often three or four. A definite must was pumpkin pie. This pie SO satisfying! It reminds me of Thanksgivings when my mom was alive.

Crust:
1 cup ground almonds
1/2 cup soy protein (NOT soy flour!)
1 teaspoon SteviaPlus®
4 packets sucralose
6 tablespoons butter

Filling:
1/2 tablespoon SteviaPlus®
6 packets sucralose
1 teaspoon salt/lite salt
2 teaspoons ground cinnamon
1 teaspoon ground ginger
1/2 teaspoon ground cloves
            (or instead of those spices use 3 1/2 teaspoons pumpkin pie
            spice, but using the individual ones really made a difference!)
4 eggs
1 - 29 oz can pumpkin
3 cups Almond Milk (see recipe, p. 145) or 2 cups cream thinned
            with water to 3 cups (but not if you have candida)

Crust instructions: Combine the crust ingredients well with a pastry blender or food processor and press the crust into a 9" pie pan.

blender or food processor and press the crust into a 9" pie pan. Place it into the refrigerator to chill while mixing the filling ingredients.

Preheat the oven to 425° F. Put the filling ingredients into a mixing bowl, putting the eggs together on one side of the bowl. Mix, using an electric mixer, mixing the eggs first then gradually incorporating them into the whole mixture. Mix until the filling is smooth.

Pour 1/2 of the filling into the pie shell, and reserve the remaining filling for later use.

The extra filling may be kept refrigerated for up to three days or frozen in a freezer container. When ready to use, simply thaw and follow crust and baking instructions.

Bake the pie at 425° F for 15 minutes. Lower the heat to 350° F for about 25 minutes. A knife inserted off center should come out clean when it is done. Serve it warm with whipped cream (but not if you have candida) or Almond Milk, (see recipe, p. 145), poured over the top. Makes two pies, one for immediate use, the other for later use, each with 8 servings.

Carb count: Entire recipe, 104.29. Fiber, 38.72. ECC, 65.57.
Entire filling, 79.38. Fiber, 24.35. ECC, 55.03.
Entire crust, 24.91. Fiber, 14.37. ECC, 10.54.
One whole pie, 63.6. Fiber 26.54. ECC, 37.06.
Per serving, 7.95. Fiber, 3.31. ECC, 4.63.

Zucchini "Bread" Patties

My daughter was the first to try Zucchini "Bread" Patties. My son blurted out as she took her first bite, "Sissy! Do they taste as yummy as they smell???" All we heard was a deep sigh and "Mmm...."

1/2 pound zucchini
1 egg
1/2 teaspoon vanilla
3/4 cup crushed pork rinds
1/2 teaspoon cinnamon
1/4 teaspoon nutmeg
1/8 teaspoon orange (or lemon) rind
1/2 teaspoon SteviaPlus®
2 packets sucralose*
1/4 cup pecan halves
Butter for cooking

Using a food processor with a shredding disk, or by hand, finely shred the zucchini. Place the shredded zucchini into a mixing bowl. Add the egg and vanilla, and mix well. In a separate bowl combine the pork rinds, cinnamon, nutmeg, orange rind, SteviaPlus® and sucralose. Mix well and add it to the zucchini mixture. Stir in the pecan halves and allow the batter to rest 3 to 5 minutes. In a skillet, melt 1 tablespoon butter over medium heat. Form the batter into 1 1/2" to 2" patties, being sure to tuck at least one pecan piece into the center of each patty. Fry them until golden on each side, about 4 minutes total. For each subsequent batch, add more butter to the pan as needed. Serve warm. 4 servings.

Carb count: Entire recipe, 9.78, Fiber, 2.32. ECC, 7.46.
Per serving, 2.44. Fiber, .58. ECC, 1.86.

Sugar-Free, Non-Low Carb Recipes

Aaron's Cookies*

*This recipe is not low carb and is not suitable for candida sufferers

I think that chocolate chip cookies were the first thing that I learned to cook. I think that my mother taught me how to bake cookies early on because she didn't want to have to do it anymore! Whatever the reason was, I learned how to make some amazing cookies. I have been told repeatedly that my cookies are better than the fancy cookies that can be purchased from fancy cookie shops! I have applied that basic cookie baking skill to a sugar-free variation. These are very chewy, soft cookies. No one even needs to know they are sugar-free!

3 1/2 cups whole wheat pastry or spelt flour
1/3 cup wheat gluten flour (or use spelt flour if wheat intolerant)
1/3 cup soy protein (NOT soy flour!)
1 teaspoon baking soda
1 teaspoon baking powder
1 1/4 cups granulated fructose
1 1/2 cups butter, room temperature
2 eggs
1 tablespoon vanilla

Additions:
2 cups total of the following: sugar-free granola, sugar-free carob/chocolate chips, nuts, dried fruit, etc...
1/2 teaspoon cinnamon (if using dried fruit, like raisins)

Pre-heat the oven to 375° F. Place a sheet of parchment paper cut to fit on each baking sheet. Place paper towels on a large flat area, like a table or counter, and cover them with waxed paper for a place to cool the cookies when they are done.

Combine the pastry flour, gluten flour, soy protein, baking soda and baking powder in a medium-sized bowl and set aside.

In a large mixing bowl, using an electric mixer on medium speed, cream the fructose and butter until light, about 2 minutes. Add the eggs and vanilla and continue to mix for another minute, until the dough is light and fluffy. Turn the speed to low and gradually add in the flour mixture by 1/4 cupfuls, making sure that each preceding addition is thoroughly combined before adding the next. When all the flour is completely incorporated, stir in the additions by hand.

Form dough into 2" balls, and place them on the parchment covered baking sheets.

When parchment paper is used, the cookies will bake to perfection and almost no clean up!

Flatten each cookie slightly with the palm of your hand. Bake them for 5 to 7 minutes at 375° F. The cookies should be just barely beginning to become golden on top. Remove them from the oven and allow them to rest on the baking sheets for one to two minutes. Place the cookies on the waxed paper cooling area and allow them to cool thoroughly.

The waxed paper over paper towels absorbs the excess moisture from the cookies and helps to produce a more pleasing cookie.

A container with a tightly fitting lid should be lined on the bottom with a paper towel. Lay the cookies in a single layer on the towel in the container. When that layer is full, add another towel and continue to place the completely cooled cookies into the container. They will store this way easily for one week and still retain their freshness. As each layer is eaten simply remove the towel to expose the next layer.

Variation:
Aaron's Chewy Jumbo Cookies: Use an ice cream scoop with a trigger, or a 1/4 cup measuring cup to scoop the dough onto the baking sheets and bake them for 8 to 10 minutes. Don't forget to flatten the tops! These Jumbo Cookies are great for extra special treats, like birthdays!

Berry Jam*

*This recipe is not low carb and is not suitable for candida sufferers

Where my family lives, in the Pacific Northwest, we have mountainous heaps of wild blackberry brambles. They grow along roadsides nearly everywhere, and are ripe for the picking in late summer. It is a simple task to fill a large, 5 gallon bucket to the top with berries after just a short amount of time, if we find a great spot to pick!

3 cups berries (blackberry, raspberry, Marion berry, loganberry, etc.)
1 1/2 cups granulated fructose
1 apple

Wash and drain the berries. Peel, core and finely chop the apple. Place the berries into a medium-sized sauce pan and crush them slightly with a potato masher. Place the remaining ingredients into the sauce pan. Bring the mixture to a boil over medium heat, stirring often. Turn the heat down to medium-low and cook for approximately one hour, stirring often, until a small amount of jam dropped on a glass dish will stay in place. Pour the jam into small plastic containers with lids leaving 1" head room. Allow the containers to rest loosely covered on the counter for 24 hours. After the resting period, seal the jam with lids, and store them either in the refrigerator for immediate use or in the freezer for later use. Makes 3 cups.

You may be thinking, "But there is no pectin! How will it ever set up???" That is what the apple is for, it contains a high amount of natural pectin. The jam sets up quite nicely!

Cheese Wrap-Ups*

*This recipe is not low carb and is not suitable for candida sufferers

My kids really like Cheese Wrap-Ups. They say they remind them of the deep fried cheese at a restaurant. I've tried to make the deep fried cheese — too much effort! These are nice and easy though!

4 commercially prepared corn tortillas
4 one-ounce sized mozzarella cheese sticks ("string cheese")

Pass the tortillas under slowly running water, so that they get thoroughly wet. Allow them to rest 2 to 3 minutes. Heat a small skillet over medium heat. Place the tortillas into the skillet one at a time until they just soften. Remove the tortillas from the heat and roll them tightly around the cheese sticks. Remove the pan from the heat. Allow the Wrap-Ups to rest 2 to 3 minutes on plates so that the tortilla won't unroll. Put the pan back onto the heat and carefully place the Wrap-Ups back into the hot skillet, turning frequently to prevent scorching, until they are becoming golden brown and the cheese inside is becoming all gooey. Makes 4 servings.

Chick in a Nest*

*This recipe is not low carb and is not suitable for candida sufferers

The first time I remember having Chick in a Nest was when my husband and I were living in New Zealand. It was a bright, sunny, hot Christmas day. (We were in the Southern Hemisphere!) Everyone had been swimming most of the afternoon or playing volleyball. We had a "barby" that evening – a bar-be-cue on a huge outdoor grill – and the family made these for everyone. Now, my kids ask for these all the time!

4 slices whole wheat or spelt bread
4 eggs
Butter
Salt and pepper to taste

Using a biscuit cutter, or a glass with a 3" opening, cut the centers out of the bread. Butter all of the pieces of bread, including the cut outs, on both sides. Place the large pieces with the holes in a large frying pan over medium heat, and put about 1/2 teaspoon butter into each hole. Break one egg into each hole and season it with salt and pepper. Cook them until the eggs are beginning to set, about 1 1/2 minutes. Flip the bread and egg over, and cook them on the other side until the toast is golden brown. Place the buttered bread cut outs into the frying pan and cook them until they are golden brown, about 30 seconds on each side. Serves 4.

Fruit Crunch*

*This recipe is not low carb and is not suitable for candida sufferers

When I was in college, I worked as a cook's helper for a retreat center in Oregon State. The large cooler and freezers were housed out in the barn. I remember walking down the path from the kitchen early in the morning, to get whatever foodstuffs were needed for the day's meals. I often took a side trip to stand and gaze at the lake in the early morning light. I loved looking out over the lake, with the mist hanging low, as it reflected the huge trees surrounding it. The frogs and crickets each made their respective music, and the barn swallows dipped low over the lake getting drinks and catching mosquitos. I learned this basic recipe while I was there at that retreat center. I have been making it for so many years, and it has changed so much; it isn't even the same thing. One thing is the same though, it still gets rave reviews whenever I make it!

Fruit filling:
8 cups ripe fruit, like blackberries, apples, peaches/nectarines, blueberries, or a combination of apples and one of the others
1/3 cup whole wheat pastry flour, spelt flour or processed rolled oats
2 tablespoons granulated fructose
1/2 tablespoon SteviaPlus®
(1/2 teaspoon cinnamon if doing apples or peaches/nectarines)
Cooking oil spray

Topping:
1 cup butter
1/2 tablespoon vanilla
1 1/4 cups whole wheat flour, spelt flour, or processed rolled oats
2 cups rolled oats
1 cup rolled rye flakes (if rye is unavailable just use rolled oats)
3/4 cup granulated fructose
1 tablespoon SteviaPlus®

To blanch fruit for peeling, bring a small pan of water to a rolling boil. Dunk the fruit into the boiling water for about 1 minute, the immersing them in another bowl with ice- cold water. Slip off the skins.

Spray a 9″x13″ baking dish with cooking oil spray. Place the prepared fruit into the baking dish. Sprinkle the remaining filling ingredients evenly over the fruit. Stir to coat the fruit evenly, if using apples or peaches/nectarines. Set aside.

Place the butter into a small microwave safe bowl and microwave on high for 1 to 2 minutes, until butter is thoroughly melted. Set aside.

In mixing bowl, place the flour, oats, rye, fructose and SteviaPlus® stirring to combine. Pour the vanilla into the bowl of melted butter, then add the butter to the flour mixture. Mix well. Carefully place the topping over the fruit in the baking dish so that it is evenly distributed. No fruit should be exposed. Bake it at 350° F for 40 to 50 minutes, or until the whole house smells wonderful and the topping has become golden brown. Serves 10.

Higher Protein French Toast*

*This recipe is not low carb and is not suitable for candida sufferers

Isn't it wonderful to be able to cook with fats again, after so many years of wimpy low-fat cooking?!?

4 eggs
2 tablespoons milk
Pinch salt (less than 1/8 teaspoon)
1/4 teaspoon SteviaPlus® or 1/2 packet sucralose
1/4 teaspoon cinnamon
6 slices whole wheat or whole spelt bread, frozen
Cooking oil (canola preferred)
Butter

In a shallow dish, combine the eggs, milk, salt, SteviaPlus® and cinnamon, mixing well. Warm about 1 tablespoon butter plus 1 tablespoon cooking oil in a large frying pan over medium heat. Dunk the slices of bread into the egg mixture, coating well. Carefully transfer them to hot frying pan. Cook them until they are golden brown on each side, adding oil as necessary to keep them from sticking to the pan.

Serve hot with butter or Nut Butter (see instructions, p. 181) and Sugar Free Pancake Syrup (see recipe, p. 58) or Berry Jam (see recipe, p. 197). Serves 3.

I serve this with Sharron's Pork Sausage (see recipe, p. 56) to give my family an extra protein edge for the day.

Huckleberry Cobbler Over a Camp-Fire*

*This recipe is not low carb and is not suitable for candida sufferers

Ever have one of those experiences with food that will be forever implanted in your memory? About two years ago, my family went camping late in the summer. I was expecting to find ripe blackberries when we got to our destination, but the campsite was ever so much different than what we had expected! The campsite was only a two hour drive from our home, which is classified as a coniferous rain forest. We have huge douglas fir trees and a high annual rainfall. The area to which we went was very arid! There were large pine trees and the dirt was a deep, loose sand. It was hot and dry. We did not find any blackberries, for they like it in damp climates. What we found instead were ripe, wild blueberries, also called huckleberries! I had brought the ingredients for a berry cobbler along with us, so I made a Huckleberry Cobbler Over a Camp-Fire. One of the yummiest foods we have ever had! My 9 year old daughter still talks about it!

Filling:
4 cups freshly picked huckleberries or other berries
2 tablespoons whole wheat pastry flour, spelt flour or processed rolled oats
1 1/2 tablespoons granulated fructose
1/8 teaspoon salt

Topping:
1 1/2 cup whole wheat pastry flour, spelt flour or processed rolled oats
1/2 cup granulated fructose
1/2 cup (one stick) butter

Other items:
Cooking oil spray
Zipper seal plastic storage bags
Foil pie pan

Empty tin can or small sauce pan
Large aluminum "turkey roaster" or foil

Be prepared ahead of time and place the flour, fructose and salt for the filling into a small plastic zipper seal bag. In a quart sized zipper sealed bag, place the flour and fructose for the topping. Take them along with you when you go camping.

While enjoying the great outdoors, discover a field full of ripe, wild huckleberries, (or other berries). Pick lots and lots of them! Return to the campsite and wash about 2 pints worth, saving the rest without washing. (If you wash the powdery-stuff off the berries, they become perishable much more quickly!) Build a campfire** in an outdoor barbecue with a grate. Allow the fire to die down to the red-hot coals stage.

Spray the pie pan with the cooking oil spray. Place the washed berries and dry filling ingredients into the pie pan, stirring lightly. Sprinkle the dry topping ingredients over the berry mixture. Melt the butter in a small pan or tin can and drizzle the butter over the topping, being careful to cover the entire top. Place the cobbler onto the grate and cover it with the turkey roaster or a foil tent and bake it for 45 minutes to 1 hour, or until the cobbler is a deep golden color and the berry juices are bubbling through.

**Or if you just want to make this in an oven, bake at 350° F for 35 to 40 minutes.

Serves 4.

Monte Christo Sandwiches*

*This recipe is not low carb and not suitable for candida sufferers

I was first introduced to Monte Christo Sandwiches when I was in college. I saw huge stacks of them in the serving counter while I was standing in the line waiting to be served. I thought they looked so weird! My roommate assured me that they were very good, though, so I tried one. It was very good! My kids call these "French toast sandwiches." They love them!

8 slices whole wheat or spelt bread
4 slices (4 ounces) Monterey Jack or Swiss cheese
(4 slices ham or turkey, optional)
3 eggs
Seasoning salt
Cooking oil (canola preferred)

Crack the eggs into a shallow dish, and beat with seasoning salt as you desire. Place approximately 1 tablespoon cooking oil into a large frying pan, and heat it over medium heat. Dip one slice of bread on one side in the egg mixture. Place the bread egg-side down in the pan. Lay cheese (and ham or turkey) on the bread. Dip another piece of bread on one side in the egg mixture and place the egg-side up on top of the sandwich. Cook for about 2 minutes per side, or until the sandwich is becoming golden brown and the cheese is melted. Repeat for the remaining sandwiches. Serve hot. Serves 4.

Piggies in a Blanket*

*This recipe is not low carb and not suitable for candida sufferers

Almost every day my kids come begging for me to make Piggies in a Blanket. It is a fun project for us all to do together!

1 1/2 cups whole wheat pastry, or spelt flour
1/4 cup wheat gluten flour (or spelt if wheat intolerant)
1/2 teaspoon salt
1 tablespoon baking powder
1/4 cup butter
3/4 cup milk
8 hot dogs
8 slices American cheese (deli-style not plastic-wrapped)

Place the flours, salt and baking powder into a mixing bowl. Place butter in bowl and using a pastry blender, or two knives, cut the butter into the flour until it resembles coarse crumbs. Pour in the milk and mix the batter until it cleans the bowl. Put a little flour on a 12" sheet of waxed paper and place the dough onto flour. Knead 10 times. Pat the dough out flat and cut into eight equal pieces. Set aside.

Cut the hot dogs into halves so that each is about 2 1/2" long. Break the cheese slices into fourths, so that each piece of cheese is about the same length as the hot dog pieces are. Set aside.

On the waxed paper, with well floured hands, pat out each piece of dough so that it is large enough to completely cover the hot dog pieces, about 3" square. Place two small cheese pieces and a hot dog half into the center of each piece of dough. Wrap the dough around the hot dog and cheese so that they are completely enclosed. Place the hot dog bundles onto a baking sheet and bake for approximately 8 minutes at 450° F. Serve hot. Serves 4.

Quesodillas*

*This recipe is not low carb and is not suitable for candida sufferers

Simple, quick and satisfying. This is a staple for quick breakfasts and lunches!

8 commercially prepared whole wheat, low carb or corn tortillas
8 slices Monterey Jack cheese

Quickly pass the tortillas under slowly running water. Set them aside for 3 minutes. Heat a large skillet over medium heat. Place one tortilla into the pan. Lay the cheese on the tortilla so that it is covered almost, but not quite, to the edge. Place another tortilla on top of the cheese. Heat the tortilla until cheese begins to melt, about 2 minutes. Flip the Quesodilla, and heat it on the other side about 1 minute. Remove it from the heat and proceed in like manner for the remaining tortillas and cheese. Cut them into wedges and serve hot. Serves 4.

Note: An ounce of sliced or chopped cooked meat may be added in with the cheese to give a higher protein level to the Quesodillas. Also, if a crisper tortilla is desired, simply spray the pan with cooking oil spray before placing the tortillas into it.

Tostadas*

*This recipe is not low carb and is not suitable for candida sufferers

My kids really enjoy it when they get to be the ones to go outside and pick the chives fresh from our garden!

4 commercially prepared tostada shells OR
        4 corn tortillas deep fried flat until crisp
1 - 16 ounce can commercially prepared refried beans
4 ounces Monterey jack cheese, shredded
1/2 cup sour cream or whole milk yogurt
1 tablespoon snipped chives
1/2 small tomato, diced
Kids' Guacamole (see recipe, p. 154) or Grown Ups' Guacamole (see recipe, p. 152) optional
Cooking oil spray

Spray a baking sheet with cooking oil spray. Place the tostada shells onto the baking sheet. Spread the refried beans evenly atop each shell. Top them with cheese. Bake them at 375° F for about 8 minutes, until cheese the is melted and bubbling. Remove them from heat and spread each with sour cream, guacamole, chives and tomato. Makes 4 servings.

Variation:
Nachos: Use plain corn tortilla chips instead of tostada shells. Place them in a 9" by 13" baking pan that has been sprayed with cooking spray. Layer with beans and cheese, and bake as directed. You may also add 1/2 pound cooked ground beef to the layers. Follow the remaining instructions as given.

Appendixes

Sample Menus

Breakfasts

Zucchini Nut Muffins, page 61
I'm Eating It So Fast Because It Is So Good, page 47

Farmer's Breakfast, page 46
Low carb Tortillas (commercially prepared)

Chubby Pancakes, page 42, or Wonderful Waffles, page 60
Sugar Free Pancake Syrup, page 58
Sharron's Pork Sausage patties, page 56

Spinach Quiche, page 57
Breaded Zucchini, page 117

Parsley Eggs with Walla Walla Sweet Sauce, page 50
1946 Pork Sausage patties, page 39

Pumpkin Waffles, page 54
Cinnamon Butter, page 43
Vanilla Sauce, page 59
Best Bacon, page 40

Omelettes With or Without Cheese, page 49
Pumpkin Spice Muffins, page 52

Lunches

Pork cutlet prepared using Kentucky-Style Seasoning,
    page 83
"Honey" Mustard Dipping Sauce, page 153
Fresh vegetables (cauliflower, broccoli, cucumber)

Rainbow Egg Salad, page 92
Celery sticks
Zucchini slices

Pork rinds (commercially prepared)

Easy Cheesy Breakfast Pizza, page 45
Tossed salad served with
Creamy Ranch Salad Dressing, page 148 and
Roasted Pumpkin Seeds, page 133

Clam Cakes, page 119
Tossed Salad served with
Creamy Roasted Garlic Salad Dressing, page 149

Cream of Broccoli Soup, page 122
Crackers, page 120
Deviled Eggs, page 124

Homemade Lunch Meat, page 92 (see tip)
Celery sticks or cabbage chunks
Rutabaga Chips, page 135

Dinners

Beef Gravy Supreme, page 68
Rice-aflower, page 132
Macadamia Nut Butter Cookies, page 181

Chunky Beef Soup, page 72
Luscious Lemon Bars, page 179

Josephine's Spicy Spaghetti Sauce, page 82
Baked Spaghetti Squash, page 115
Mmm Cookies, page 184

Wonderful Chicken Club Pizza, page 112
Yummy Coleslaw, page 164
Coconut Macaroons, page 172

Seven Hills Chili, page 96
Meringue Kisses, page 183

Beef Stew with Pumpkin, page 69
Zucchini "Bread" Patties, page 192

Special Occasions

Egg Rolls, page 126
Barbecue Pork, page 67
Roasted Garlic, page 157
Sweet and Sour Sauce, Low Carbed, page 162
Fiery Hot Mustard, page 150
Sesame seeds
Lemon Chess Custard, page 178

Lemony Beef and Asparagus Stir-Fry, page 85
Rice-aflower, page 132
Ultimate Pumpkin Pie, page OR 190
Pumpkin Cheesecake, page 186 (not if you have candida)

Sole Almondine, page 97
Spinach Salad with Lemon Dressing, page 161
Meringue Kisses, page 183 OR
Melt In Your Mouth Mousse, page 182 (not if you have candida)

Elegant Chicken, page 77 (not if you have candida)
French-Style Green Beans, page 130
Creamy Delicious Cheesecake, 173 page (not if you have candida)

Bon-Fire Barbecue Steak, page 70
Roasted Veggies Over a Bon-Fire, page 134
Huckleberry Cobbler Over a Camp-Fire, page 203
        (non-low carb) OR
Mmm Cookies, page 184

Steam Boat, page 99
Aimee's Original French Silk Pie, page 167

Extra Special Egg Nog, page 175 (not if you have candida)
Roast Leg of Lamb, page 93
Baked Winter Squash, page 115
Coconut Silk Pie, page 189

Salmon Patties, page 94
Tartar Sauce, page 163
Slurp 'Em Up Cabbage Noodles, page 138
Cast of Thousands on Many Continents Chocolate Cake,
    page 169 with
Chocolate Cream Cheese Frosting, page 171

Kids' Stuff

Teeny Food, page 107
Meringue Kisses, page 183

Quesodillas, page 207
Celery filled with
Nut Butter, page 181

Monte Christo Sandwiches, page 205
Luscious Lemon Bars, page 179

Easy Cheesy Breakfast Pizza, page 45
Breaded Summer Squash, page 117
Aaron's Cookies, page 195 made with oatmeal and raisins

Tostadas or Nachos, page 208
Baby carrots
Aaron's Cookies, page 195 made with carob chips

Piggies in a Blanket, page 206
Zucchini "Bread" Patties, page 192

Suggested Shopping List

Sweeteners:
> SteviaPlus® (the 4 ounce shaker bottle preferred, but the packets may be substituted)
> Sucralose packets

Meats:
> Eggs
> Beef
> Chicken
> Pork
> Fish
> Etc..... (Try to use the best quality fresh meat available)

Oils and Fats:
> Butter
> Canola oil
> Sunflower oil
> Canola oil cooking spray
> Olive oil

Ethnic cookery items:
> Soy sauce (but not if you have candida!)
> Sesame oil
> Hot chili oil
> Sesame seeds
> Tomato sauce (without sugar)
> Canned tomatoes (without sugar)
> Chili powder, chilies OR jalapeno peppers
> Cumin (ground)
> Italian seasoning herb blend
> Low carb tortillas (optional, and not if you have candida!)

Fruits and vegetables:
> Lemons
> Limes
> Bottled lemon juice
> Cabbage
> Spinach (pre-washed bagged is nice!)
> Rutabagas

Celery
Cauliflower
Zucchini
Cucumber
Radishes
Green beans (canned, frozen or fresh)
Olives (canned, black)

Nuts:
Raw almonds
Blanched almonds (optional)
Sunflower seeds
Macadamia nuts
Ground macadamia nuts (optional)

Herbs, seasonings and miscellany:
Seasoning salt (without sugar)
Lemon pepper (without sugar)
Garlic salt or granules
Mustard powder
Ground ginger
Dried onions
Dried parsley
Dried chives (or fresh if available)
Rosemary
Lemon thyme (or regular thyme)
Mint (if no dried mint is available, use mint tea bags)
Garlic
Onions
Cinnamon
Vanilla (real vanilla extract, not imitation!)
Almond extract
Arrowroot powder
Guar gum (if available)
Soy protein (in the beverages section at most grocers)
Pork rinds

Items for sugar free, wheat free cookery:
Granulated fructose
Whole oats
Spelt flour
Rye flour (optional)

Carb Counts of Common Foods

Please note, all information presented was taken from the USDA Agricultural Research Service Nutrient Data Laboratory http://www.nal.usda.gov/fnic/cgi-bin/nut_search.pl

ITEM	CARBS	FIBER	ECC
Almonds, blanched, 1 cup	28.91	15.08	13.83
Almond, whole raw, 1 nut	.23	.14	.09
Almonds, ground, 1 cup	18.75	11.21	7.54
Almonds, whole raw, 1 cup	28.03	16.75	11.28
Arrowroot powder, 1 tablesp.	7.05	.27	6.78
Asparagus, spear (6")	.72	.33	.39
Avocado, whole	14.85	10.05	4.80
Baking chocolate, 1 ounce	8.02	4.36	3.66
Baking powder, 1 teaspoon	1.27	trace	1.27
Baking soda, 1 teaspoon	0	0	0
Basil, 1 teaspoon	.85	.56	.29
Beans, green, 1 cup	7.85	3.74	4.11
Beans, green, 1 pound	32.42	15.44	16.97
Broccoli, 1 cup chopped	4.61	2.64	1.97
Cabbage, chopped, 1 cup	4.83	2.04	2.79
Cabbage, shredded, 1 cup	3.80	1.61	2.19
Cabbage, whole, medium	49.30	20.88	28.42
Carrot, medium (5.5")	7.3	2.16	5.14
Cauliflower, whole, medium	29.9	14.37	15.53
Celery, large stalk (12")	2.33	1.08	1.25
Celery seed, 1 teaspoon	.82	.23	.59
Cheese, Cheddar, 1 cup, gr.	1.44	n/a	1.44
Cheese, cream, 1 ounce	.75	n/a	.75
Cheese, cream, 1 tablespoon	.38	n/a	.38
Cheese, Monterey, 1 cup, gr.	.76	n/a	.76
Cheese, Mozzarella, 1 cup, gr.	3.54	n/a	3.54
Cheese, Mozzarella, 1 ounce	.89	n/a	.89
Cheese, Parmesan, 1 tablesp.	.18	n/a	.18
Cheese, Swiss, 1 cup, grated	3.65	n/a	3.65
Chili powder, 1 teaspoon	1.42	.88	.54
Chives, 1 teaspoon	.04	.02	.02
Cinnamon, 1 teaspoon	1.83	1.24	.59
Cloves, ground, 1 teaspoon	1.28	.71	.57

ITEM	CARBS	FIBER	ECC
Cocoa powder, 1 tablespoon	2.93	1.79	1.14
Coconut, unsweetened 1/2 c.	10	7	3
Cornstarch, 1 tablespoon	7.3	.07	7.23
Cream, half & half, 1 cup	10.4	n/a	10.4
Cream, whipping, 1 cup	6.64	n/a	6.64
Cream of tartar, 1 teaspoon	1.84	trace	1.84
Cumin, 1 teaspoon	.92	.22	.7
Dill weed, 1 teaspoon	.55	.13	.42
Egg, white, large	.34	n/a	.34
Egg, whole, large	.61	n/a	.61
Fennel, 1 teaspoon	1.04	.79	.25
Garlic, 1 clove	.99	.06	.93
Garlic powder, 1 teaspoon	2.03	.27	1.76
Ginger, ground, 1 teaspoon	1.27	.22	1.05
Guar gum, 1 tsp. (from pkg.)	2.5	2.5	0
Lemon peel, 1 teaspoon	.32	.21	.11
Lemon juice, fresh 1 cup	21.05	.97	20.08
Lemon juice, fresh, 2 tbsp.	2.63	.12	2.51
Lemon juice, bottled, 1 cup	15.81	.97	14.84
Lemon juice, bottled, 1 tbsp.	.98	.06	.92
Lemon thyme, 1 teaspoon	.19	.11	.08
Lime juice, 2 tablespoons	2.77	.12	2.65
Macadamia nuts, 1 cup	18.51	11.52	6.99
Macadamia nuts, 1 ounce	3.79	2.26	1.53
Marjoram, 1 teaspoon	.36	.24	.12
Mint leaves, 2 tablespoons	.47	.25	.22
Mushroom, medium	.73	.21	.52
Mustard seed, 1 teaspoon	1.15	.48	.67
Nutmeg, 1 teaspoon	1.08	.45	.63
Oats, 1 cup dry	54.27	8.58	45.69
Okra, 1 cup	7.63	3.2	4.43
Olive, 1 large	.27	.14	.13
Onion flakes, dried, 1 tablesp.	4.16	.46	3.7
Onion, fresh, 1 cup chopped	13.8	2.88	10.92
Onion, fresh, medium	9.49	1.98	7.51
Onion, green, medium (4.5")	1.10	.39	.71
Orange peel, 1teaspoon	.50	.21	.29
Oregano, ground 1 teaspoon	.96	.64	.32
Paprika, 1 teaspoon	1.17	.43	.74
Parsley, dried, 1 tablespoon	.67	.39	.28
Peanut butter, 2 tablespoons	6.17	1.88	4.29

ITEM	CARBS	FIBER	ECC
Peas, frozen, 1 cup	9.86	3.38	6.48
Pecan halves, 1 cup	14.96	10.36	4.6
Pepper, bell, medium	7.65	2.14	5.51
Pepper, black, 1 teaspoon	1.36	.55	.81
Pepper, cayenne, 1 teaspoon	1.01	.49	.52
Pepper, chili, dried	.37	.15	.22
Pepper, jalapeno	.82	.39	.43
Pumpkin, canned, 1 cup	19.79	7.1	12.69
Pumpkin seeds, 1 cup	24.57	5.38	19.19
Radish, 1 medium	.16	.07	.09
Rosemary, 1 teaspoon	.14	.09	.05
Rutabaga, small	15.61	4.8	10.81
Sage, 1 teaspoon	.42	.28	.14
Sesame seeds, 1 tablespoon	2.11	1.06	1.05
Sour cream, 1 cup	9.82	n/a	9.82
Soy flour, 1 tablespoon	1.83	.49	1.34
Soy protein, 1 ounce (1/4 c.)	2.08	1.58	.5
Spaghetti squash, 1 cup	10.01	2.17	7.84
Spinach, 1 cup	1.05	.81	.24
Squash, winter, 1 cup	17.93	5.74	12.19
Sunflower seeds, 1 tablesp.	1.72	.96	.75
Thyme, fresh, 1 teaspoon	.19	.11	.08
Tomato, medium	5.7	1.35	4.35
Tomato sauce, 1 cup	17.59	3.43	14.16
Tomatoes, canned, 1 cup	10.48	2.4	8.08
Turnip, small	3.8	1.09	2.71
Vanilla, 1 teaspoon	.53	n/a	.53
Walnuts, 1 cup chopped	15.12	6.25	8.87
Waterchestnuts, 1/2 cup sl.	8.7	1.75	6.95
Zucchini, medium	5.68	2.35	3.33
Zucchini, 1 cup chopped	3.59	1.48	2.11

Conversion Chart for Sugar Substitutes Used in This Book

SUCRALOSE
I use the Splenda™ No Calorie Sweetener brand of sucralose product. Each packet weighs 1 gram.

1 packet = 2 teaspoons sugar
3 packets = 2 tablespoons sugar
6 packets = 1/4 cup sugar
8 packets = 1/3 cup sugar
12 packets = 1/2 cup sugar
24 packets = 1 cup sugar

STEVIA
I use the brand SteviaPlus® (www.wisdomherbs.com). Because I blend it with another sweetener, the sweetness ratio is approximately 30 times sweeter than sugar. It is a stevia extract that is a fine white powder combined with a healthy dietary fiber called FOS. It is my understanding that FOS helps stabilize blood sugar levels. The FOS also makes this product milder and easier to cook with than other stevia products. Other brands of stevia may not have the same conversion values.

1 tablespoon stevia = 2 cups sugar
1/2 tablespoon stevia = 1 cup sugar
1 teaspoon stevia = 2/3 cup sugar
3/4 teaspoon stevia = 1/2 cup sugar
1/2 teaspoon stevia = 1/3 cup sugar
1/4 teaspoon stevia = 2 1/2 tablespoons sugar
1/8 teaspoon stevia = 1 tablespoon plus 1/2 teaspoon sugar

SweetLeaf™ Company Product Equivalencies

Sugar	SteviaPlus® Fiber Packets	SteviaPlus® Fiber Powder	SteviaClear™ Liquid Stevia
1 teaspoon	1/2 packet	1/4 teaspoon	2 to 3 drops
2 teaspoons	1 packet	1/2 teaspoon	4 to 6 drops
1 tablespoon	1 1/2 to 2 packets	3/4 teaspoon	6 to 9 drops
1 cup	18 to 24 packets	1 1/2 to 2 tablespoons	1 teaspoon
2 cups	36 to 48 packets	3 to 4 tablespoons	2 teaspoons

Sugar	Stevia Extract Powder	Stevia Concentrate Dark Liquid	HoneyLeaf™ Stevia Leaf Powder
1 teaspoon	n/a	4 to 6 drops	n/a
2 teaspoons	n/a	8 to 12 drops	n/a
1 tablespoon	n/a	1/8 teaspoon	1/4 teaspoon
1 cup	1/3 to 1/2 teaspoon	1 tablespoon	1 1/2 to 2 tablespoons
2 cups	2/3 to 1 teaspoon	2 tablespoons	3 to 4 tablespoons

I use SteviaPlus® Fiber Powder in my recipes, but Stevia is available in these other forms from the SweetLeaf™ Company (www.wisdomherbs.com). All equivalencies are approximate. Adjust according to your taste. Other brands of stevia may not have the same conversion values.

Bibliography

Atkins, Robert C. M.D., Dr. Atkin's New Diet Revolution. Avon Books: New York, NY 1992, 1999.

Better Homes and Gardens New Cook Book. Meredith Corporation: Des Moines, IA 1981, 1987.

Crook, William G., Chronic Fatigue and the Yeast Connection, Professional Books, Jackson, TN 1992.

Ortman, Mark, A Simple Guide to Self-Publishing. Wise Owl Books: Kirkland, WA 1994.

Rombauer, Irma S. and Rombauer-Becker, Marion, Joy of Cooking. Bobbs-Merrill Company: Indidanapolis, IN 1931, 1975.

Wolfe, J. Kevin, You Can Write a Cookbook. Writer's Digest Books: Cincinnati, OH 2000.

Thank You!!!

I just wanted to say "thank you" to all the various folks who have helped me along the way!

First of all, I need to thank Leo Pena who was the one who urged me on to do this book! Without his insistence, I never would have taken this leap of faith.

I also need to profusely thank Andrea Mondello, the owner of www.lowcarbeating.com, who showed profound trust in me by asking me to write a cooking column for her website and has provided unlimited encouragement and support!

Special thanks to Steve May at Wisdom Herbs (www.wisdomherbs.com), the maker of SteviaPlus®, and to Mike Small, his assistant for their incredible support of this project. I would not have been able to do it without them.

I need to thank my sister, Susan Yates, for being my cooking resource person and all around best friend. She provided many recipes for this book and helped test and develop several others, not to mention the huge undertaking of helping with all the carb counting! Whenever I have a question about cooking techniques, I know who to call!

A big "Thank you!" to my family who endured my endless recipe testing and kept my courage up with their positive feedback.

Special thanks to all the folks who have tested recipes for me: Carolyne Radon, Connie Pritchett, Roger Ebner, Stephanie Gabinet-Bethoulle, Vicki Dewald, Penny Quinn, Kim Debus, Jennifer Paske, DJ Rosales, Kelly Clark and countless others from the www.lowcarbeating.com community who have tried recipes for me. Also, a general thanks to the www.lowcarbeating.com community for providing me great feedback and support during the times that haven't been so easy. Thank you for being such a great bunch of folks!

Of course, I need to thank the Lord for enabling me to accomplish this task. My life is nothing without Him.